S0-DQY-296

CAMPIE

CAMPIE

1 a sober, celibate, bankrupt vegetarian who mops floors, cleans toilets, burns garbage, does laundry, makes beds and picks up after rig workers. **2** nickname for the camp attendant in an oil-rig camp. **3** the loneliest person in the oil fields.

BARBARA STEWART

VICTORIA | VANCOUVER | CALGARY

Copyright © 2011 Barbara Stewart

All rights reserved. No part of this publication may be reproduced, stored in a retrieval system or transmitted in any form or by any means—electronic, mechanical, audio recording or otherwise—without the written permission of the publisher or a photocopying licence from Access Copyright, Toronto, Canada.

Heritage House Publishing Company Ltd.
www.heritagehouse.ca

LIBRARY AND ARCHIVES CANADA CATALOGUING IN PUBLICATION

Stewart, Barbara, 1954–
   Campie / Barbara Stewart.

Issued also in electronic format.
ISBN 978-1-926613-92-5

   1. Stewart, Barbara, 1954–. 2. Women cleaning personnel—Alberta—Biography.
3. Women oil industry workers—Alberta—Biography. 4. Camps—Employees—Biography.
5. Petroleum workers—Dwellings—Alberta. I. Title.

HD8039.C442C3 2011   331.4'816485097123   C2010-907924-8

Edited by Audrey McClellan
Proofread by Liesbeth Leatherbarrow
Cover and book design by Jacqui Thomas
Cover photos by Jim Jurica/iStockphoto.com; background painting by JuanFMora/
   iStockphoto.com

The interior of this book was produced using 100% post-consumer recycled paper, processed chlorine free and printed with vegetable-based inks.

Heritage House acknowledges the financial support for its publishing program from the Government of Canada through the Canada Book Fund (CBF), Canada Council for the Arts and the province of British Columbia through the British Columbia Arts Council and the Book Publishing Tax Credit.

  Canadian Patrimoine
Heritage canadien

 The Canada Council | Le Conseil des Arts
for the Arts | du Canada

 BRITISH COLUMBIA
ARTS COUNCIL

Printed in Canada

14 13 12 11   1 2 3 4

To Marguerite W.—Great events did come to pass.

CONTENTS

QUESNEL TO CHETWYND

As I made the icy turns to the summit, a sense of awe came over me. Night clouds broke apart over the frozen shrouded beauty. Dark fragments of earth rose in torn moonlit peaks. I knew, even in my fear, that I was moving through more than just Pine Pass, British Columbia. For hours I had driven terrified of sliding off the road. Now my shoulders loosened and something inside me let go. This was how to drive blind into the future: life could end at the next corner. My hands clenched the wheel. What a backdrop to those white knuckles, the moving white road and the moving black night. *Your life is in your hands.*

After the summit, the long descent: signs marked the distance to Chetwynd and a bed for the night. An elk leapt out of the dark, onto the road, and as quickly bounced off. The animal was bigger than the car. My eyes burned. I'd driven 300 kilometres non-stop from Quesnel. Only 20 kilometres left to go. My calf muscles cramped. The white road tried to hypnotize me. Every few minutes I cranked the car window open and blasted icy air onto my face.

Abruptly, the wilderness ended and the snow-packed road widened into civilized streetlights and a row of motels. The small of my back screamed for joy. I slowed to read the neon signs—NO VACANCY NO VACANCY NO VACANCY—one after the other, until I ran out of town. *I'm sleeping in my car?* Panic tightened my chest. I turned the car around and drove the row again until I spotted the only VACANCY. For all I had asked of the dear old Toyota Tercel that night, braving treacherous roads and big bully semis, I did not want to ask it to be my bed.

I pulled in beside the motel office. A small white sign was propped in the window: JESUS IS LORD. A bell rang when I pushed through the door. A man came out to the desk, rubbing his eyes. He took my cash and gave me a key.

"Rucky—rast room reft," he said.

I got the last parking spot too, sliding on the ice between hefty four-wheel-drive crew cabs tethered to electrical outlet posts. The Toyota didn't have a block heater. When did I ever need one back home in balmy Victoria? The car had over 369,000 kilometres on the motor, the dash lights didn't work and neither did the radio or turn signals, except on a lucky bump. I had driven all the way with a flashlight gripped between my knees so I could see the speedometer and gas gauge.

The last thing I'd done before leaving Quesnel earlier that day was stop at Wal-Mart to buy headlights; I'd been driving for weeks with only high beams. *What if something else breaks down?* I could only pray for God's travelling mercies: "We're going for a long drive and you're coming with me." Then I'd stuck my arm out the window to hand-signal a turn north onto Highway 97 and the start of my journey. It was 5:30 p.m., Monday, January 13, 2003.

Five hours later I turned the car headlights off in the Chetwynd motel parking lot. The keys were still in the ignition. *Will it start again?*

Welfare in Quesnel had given me $760, a one-time emergency allowance that included extra for work clothes and travel expenses to my new job. An accident or a breakdown wouldn't take long to eat that up. It was all the money I had in the world—no credit cards or even a cellphone. Thanks to my mother, the car had new snow tires, not the best, but decent. I'd never been north of Prince George and didn't know what to expect of the roads ahead. Back in Quesnel, Uncle Clifford had inked the route on a map while Aunty Madge made up a thermos of coffee and a couple of ham-and-cheese buns for the trip. Then she'd handed me a white candle, a blue Bic lighter and a rag.

"If you go off the road, use the gas from your tank to set your spare tire on fire and stay alive," she explained.

Now I was too exhausted to care. *Good luck, car.* I unfolded my wooden legs and hauled my suitcase out of the trunk. The plastic wheels crunched across the ruts, the only sound in the frozen parking lot. Not a single room light was on in the building. *Early bedtime?* My room was plain brown and ice cold. I found the thermostat and cranked the old dial over as far as it would go. Then I made the promised phone call to Aunty Madge in Quesnel.

"Okay, hon." Her voice was sleepy. "Call us tomorrow when you get to Grande Prairie."

We said goodnight and I turned from the phone to the suitcase. The clothes inside were too cold from the trunk, so no pajamas. Instead I pulled on another pair of socks and climbed into the bed fully dressed. The quilt was paper-thin, the wrapper around the fudgsicle. *I'm here.* Knees tight to my chest, I watched the fireworks behind my eyelids and listened to a lullaby of tire rubber on road snow and ice. *I'm cold.* The antique wall heater gurgled and bonged to mark the miraculous occasion of my safe arrival. *I'm alive.*

CHETWYND TO TRINIDAD 11

The plate glass window beside the bed was vibrating. At 4:00 a.m., every diesel engine in the parking lot fired up and pulled out. I wasn't far behind, bumpy suitcase in tow. The Toyota looked like a frosty bloodstain on the vacant ice. This kind of cold was new to me: killer cold. *What if the car is dead?* I put the key in the ignition, took a deep breath and prayed. It started. *Unbelievable.* While the motor wheezed, thick snow started to fall, the wind whipping it up at the same time it was coming down. Back out on the highway, pickup trucks and semi-trailers easily shouldered their way around and passed me on blind corners and single-lane hills. As the day lightened, I realized that dark-ness had served as a good blinder—the cliffs I couldn't see didn't terrify me. Daylight driving was actually harder. Three and a half tense hours later, I arrived at Grande Prairie, Alberta.

It was a big city on the move—not what I had expected to find in the north. The Toyota bobbed like a cork between deep channels of chewed snow. This city, unlike Victoria, knew the business end of a plough. First thing, I found a pay phone and left a message for

Aunty Madge, my words recorded like crumbs over Pine Pass. Next, I followed my new employer's directions to the rendezvous point, the Prairie Haven Motel. Like most businesses, it was cupped by snowbanks the size of ski hills.

It's not too late. You can still turn around and go back.

I knew I wouldn't go back. Six weeks earlier, I'd left Victoria, broke and homeless, to stay with family in Quesnel. *When it all goes south, you can always go north.* Everybody knew that—a guy could always get a job in the north. But when I couldn't find work in Quesnel, short of Tim Horton's, I looked farther north. Too bad I wasn't a guy.

I was a divorced 48-year-old backslidden Anglican, a sober, celibate vegetarian, recently discharged from bankruptcy. In three short years I'd gone from a clear-title homeowner in Victoria to homeless. My life, whatever had survived the bankruptcy, was now a pile of boxes in my uncle's Quesnel basement.

After weeks of searching for work, Legacy Industrial Camps had hired me to work as a camp attendant at an oil rig about 100 kilometres southwest of Grande Prairie. The camp job was the alternative to my prayer: "Dear God, please kill me."

A man named Jason had interviewed me on the phone. Although I'd never worked in a camp before, I told him that I'd done similar work—I knew how to wash floors and clean bathrooms—I *really* wanted the job. Then he said he'd see what he could *come up* with . . .

Did he lick the phone?

"Call me Friday," he'd said.

I did.

"Call me Monday," he'd teased.

I did.

"Can you be in Grande Prairie by noon tomorrow?"

"Absolutely. I'll be there."

He rambled on about what Legacy expected of me and said something about after-hours behaviour with the men in camp, but I could barely hear him over my pounding heart. I was to meet Stan, the camp cook, at the Prairie Haven Motel in Grande Prairie. "Stan will bring you into camp from there," he ended.

And now I was here, right on time. The Prairie Haven restaurant was filling up with lunch customers, broad-chested men in overalls and company jackets—exotic fare compared to the trim Victoria civil servants in neon bike tights that I was accustomed to seeing. I chose a table near the front door. It was almost 12 o'clock. Stan should be here any minute. Every time the door opened and a man walked in alone, I looked up expectantly, my face filled with longing and hope, the incarnation of a country ballad. Too nervous to eat, I explained to the waitress that I was supposed to meet someone. My stomach cramped—*diarrhea!* I was afraid to go to the bathroom and miss Stan. An hour passed. More coffee, no Stan.

I fiddled with napkins, chewed gum, opened the curtain beside my table. A life-sized wooden nativity scene was still set up in the snow. An angel perched on a stable over Mary, Joseph and baby Jesus. Around them were the three wise men, a donkey, a cow and a camel. The wall dissolved and I became part of the scene, an offering of grilled cheese sandwiches and chicken noodle soup. Men came and left while I watched and waited for my life to change.

Finally, at two o'clock, I left the table and phoned Legacy Industrial Camps. Maybe I had the wrong instructions. The office put me on hold.

With the phone to my ear, I overheard the waitress say, "Yes, there was a woman waiting around here . . ."

Quickly I leaned around the corner and saw her talking to a small-framed man, maybe five foot five and 150 pounds. He had a fresh haircut. My heart jumped.

"It's me," I called and waved. "I'm the woman you're waiting for—I'm on the phone with Legacy. I was told to meet you here at noon." At the same time, Jason came on the line and asked if Stan was there yet. "Yes, he just walked in," I said and handed the phone to Stan.

"It's not my fault. Don't you guys talk to each other?" Stan said loudly. "I told Mark I'd be here at two."

While he was talking, I sized him up. Stan wore a fleece-lined denim jacket that matched his indigo blue jeans—a size I figured wouldn't pull up past my size 14 hips. His short straight hair was greyish yellow. He was clean-shaven, no moustache, no earrings, his only accessory was a wristwatch that didn't look expensive. Overall, Stan appeared to be fading. His skin and teeth had the sallow tan of late-night television and a diet of all-white vegetables. In particular, I noticed that he was missing his upper left cuspid.

I'm going to leave here with a stranger to go somewhere I've never been. No one knows where I'm going or how long I'll be gone.

My belly cramped again, adding its voice to the last-minute argument. Was the job worth a mug shot on the provincial list of missing women?

This job is my survival.

Stan waved me over as he hung up the phone. He looked annoyed. I pasted a smile on my face and wondered if I could take him in a fight.

"They told me you were coming by bus," he said, running his hand through his hair. "We gotta get going."

"Okay. Where can I leave my car?"

"Oh, just park it next door. It'll be fine there." He pointed toward the Trumpeter Hotel next door.

I parked the car in the middle of the Trumpeter parking lot and hoped it would be overlooked in the rows of trucks. Maybe the hotel had some agreement with Legacy, but I didn't ask. Maybe the police would find the car if they never found me. *Should I leave a note on the dash?*

No time. Stan pulled up in his truck. I yanked the suitcase and my cousin Darlene's boots out of the trunk. *Rats.* I'd been dreaming of floating out to camp in one of those new crew cabs that were every-where. This truck was something from the early '80s, a dinged-up GMC the same worn-out blue as Stan's eyes.

"There's no room in front. Pass me that stuff and I'll put it in the back." He heaved my suitcase into the mud and snow slopping around in the open box of the truck. My books and wallet were in my back-pack. *No way.* I gripped the pack to my chest and climbed into the cab. He got in behind the wheel and stepped on the gas. "We'll be there in about an hour."

Get him talking. I asked him about camp life and the kind of work I would be doing. He spoke easily; his tone calmed me. He said he was just back from a year in Chad, Africa, where he had cooked every day at a camp for about 1,500 people. As for my own job, he had a few tips.

"Andy will show you the ropes. He's the campie you're relieving." Then, seeing the question on my face, he added, "That's what we call the camp attendant—campie. Don't let him put you off. He's just a little rough," Stan explained. "But if you're going to get, you know, *friendly* with the men, could you just try to be a little discreet about it? The last camp I was at, all hell was breaking out over this woman. What a mess." He rolled his eyes.

"I'm just here to do a job," I answered quickly. "I don't get *friendly* with people I work with—it's not a good idea."

Is friendly part of my job?

"Oh good," Stan said, though he sounded sure all hell was going to break out again. "But just so you know."

We were driving south on Highway 40. Every so often, Stan would mutter and slow at a turnoff. He had to lift himself up to look over the steering wheel at my side of the road. I wasn't sure what he was looking for until we both saw a cluster of wooden markers anchored in the snow on the side of the highway.

"There it is," he said. "That's the flag for the North Weyer-haeuser Road." He slowed the truck to make the right turn off the highway. "This note says to drive nine kilometres to a triangle and stay right onto Nose Mountain Road to marker 6-88. Then follow the signs to Trinidad 11." He held up a crumpled piece of torn-off paper in his hand.

My life is not in my hands.

We turned onto the packed snow and gravel road into a white wilderness maze. Every intersection sprouted a crop of markers, like fence pickets with multicolored flags and arrows, all sizes and shapes. Each camp and drilling company had its own directional markers. Sometimes there'd be 20 or more, all at crazy angles in the snow, some knocked over, the smaller obscured by the larger. While we tried to sort them out from the safety of the cab, traffic erupted from the trees— prehistoric traffic, trucks misshapen by their sheer size, dinosaurs with windshield eyes and chrome jaws.

"This way," Stan said and gunned the truck into the melee. It stalled. In a flash he hopped out, threw up the hood, stabbed the motor with a screwdriver, slammed the hood and split my eardrums. He was back at the wheel before I could scream.

"Look for Legacy Camp or Trinidad 11," Stan said, turning the engine over.

I thought I heard an odd twist of blame in his voice.

We drove on. Fuel trucks passed us on tight corners, and company crew cabs peppered the hood of Stan's truck with ice and gravel. I lost all sense of north and south in the unbroken uniformity of frozen white trees. The only landmarks I saw were a radio tower, an oil rig and another camp that Stan called "Beaver." It was hopeless. I knew I'd never find my way back out alone, in daylight or dark—not even with a map. The road was nine kilometres of switchbacks, breakaways, double-crosses and unmarked spurs.

An animal ran out on the road. At first I thought it was a deer. No, maybe a big dog. No, a . . .

"A wolf," said Stan.

I wanted to ask Stan more about the camp, but the drive held his attention.

"Here's home," he said suddenly, his voice full of relief. The road curved into a large clearing and he pulled up in front of a low square building on a graded flat. He parked between a dozen or so shiny four-wheel-drive crew cabs.

"We'll get the stuff later—come in and meet everybody," he said over his shoulder.

I jumped out and followed him to the door. The building was actually four brown Atco trailers linked side by side. Stan hopped up three giant plank steps and left the door open for me. I took a deep breath and went inside.

The first thing was the smell: the air was old, worn out, all used up and dense with cigarette smoke. The second thing was the heat. This air needed to be shovelled out an open window.

"Here's the kitchen," said Stan, striding at a smart clip. "And here's Andy."

Oh yes, Andy was a character, I could see that right away. Somewhere in his 60s, Andy was a stout bowlegged man built around a beach-ball belly. His wiry grey hair stood up for a fight. Three things hung solidly on his lip: a Scottish accent, a cigarette and the word "fuck." He said I'd have no trouble getting the hang of the fucking job. After two days, I'd have the fucking hang of it. He had been in camp for 49 fucking days straight and I was his fucking relief.

Lil, the outgoing cook, and Isabel, the cook's helper, were leaving camp today with Andy. Isabel's relief was another new woman coming in with the grocery supply truck. It was already hours late. I figured out that the late truck was their ride back to Grande Prairie. Duffle bags were stacked like an inukshuk at the kitchen door.

"Come on, Barb," said Stan "We're having a meeting to find out what's going on here." He waved at me through shifting layers of smoke.

I followed him to the room labelled *Cook*. There were two bunks on either side of the room, a desk centred under a window. Lil was sitting with Stan on one side; Andy had dragged in a chair. I joined Isabel, perched on the edge of the other bunk. Stupidly, I had put on a bright yellow running jacket that morning. Doubly dumb were my running tights and running shoes. I looked like a big canary.

They used Legacy matches to light four fresh cigarettes. While the talk went on about things I didn't understand, I studied the other women. Now Stan's pallor made sense. Camp life had sucked the pigment out of all of them. Lil, maybe in her late 60s, had muddled grey hair and the hobbled gait of a seized back. She was shapeless, a woman hard labour had worn down to knuckles and feet. Her helper, Isabel, was a First Nations woman I guessed to be in her early 40s; she was missing a lot of weight and most of her teeth. Her tight white blouse was unbuttoned deeply to show protruding bones, not breasts.

The two women punctuated their gestures with cigarettes in the grip of clenched fists. Weeks ago I'd heard someone back in Quesnel say that oil-rig camps preferred to hire women because they stuck with this kind of work. Based on what I saw here, it seemed to make men out of them.

"Andy, why don't you show Barb the ropes," said Stan.

"Sure, I'll give you the tour," Andy said and jerked his head for me to follow him.

We walked back to the main door. He explained how all the rooms opened off one main hallway, a square within the square building. The camp attendant's bedroom was beside the main camp door and directly across from the kitchen. The Rec Room was across from the bedrooms, each one labelled for the jobs of the men who'd sleep there: Derrickmen, Drillers, Motormen.

We turned left, the first corner. Leasehand and Roughneck rooms were on the right, across from the three bathrooms. Each stretch of hallway, about 4 feet wide, was the length of an Atco trailer, just over 50 feet. We made another left turn. Laundry and ladies' bathroom were on the left, across the hall from the bedrooms for the cook and cook's helper. Next, the Pantry Room: it had three 22-cubic-foot chest freezers and a wall of storage shelves and vegetable bins.

The third hallway turned directly into the kitchen, the largest room in camp, an entire trailer length. A long row of cupboards on the inside wall hung over three industrial-sized sinks. A heavy coil sprayer with a nozzle the size of a cauliflower dangled from the taps. Two massive refrigerators anchored each end of the kitchen. Directly across from the sinks was a steel-hooded half acre stove with a three-plate grill. The deep fryer was separate from the stove and big enough to sizzle a cow whole. Blocks of knives idled on a runway of counter space. Near the door where we'd started the tour, at the far end of the kitchen, three long chrome tables lined up for the business of feeding the crew. Finally, the outside kitchen wall was a solid row of windows to snow, trees, sky and absolutely nothing else.

Andy had walked the square and returned to the main camp door. He looked at his watch. It was time to begin my campie training.

"The bedrooms are the priority," said Andy. "Leave everything else, but make sure you get the rooms done. It shouldn't take more than two minutes to do each room." He pulled a wooden doorstop from his pocket. "And when you go into a room, always wedge the door open," he snorted, "so no one thinks anything's going on in there. Don't forget—wedge open the door." He opened the Roughnecks door and showed me how to ram the wedge with my foot. The room oozed a hot sauce of ripe feet.

All the bedrooms were set up the same way: two single beds with a desk between them. A window with blinds, the skinny plastic slats always closed. Andy demonstrated how to make up the bed, a single vinyl mattress set into a wooden box frame.

"First, you yank everything off the bed. But if he's left anything on it, any fucking clothes, leave it. Don't make it. They fucking know better. So as long as there's nothing on the bed but blankets, you yank everything off in one pull. Keep it all together so you can heave it all back in one throw."

I was impressed. Andy had a system.

"Then you lift the mattress up over the edge of the box frame so it's sitting at an angle. Throw the bottom sheet like this, over the mattress, and grab the far edge with both hands." As he said this, with a sharp movement he lifted the mattress and let it drop. The vacuum action sucked the bottom sheet underneath and held it tight when the mattress fell back into place. Next he added the top sheet, blanket and pillow. Snap, smooth, fold, done.

"Wipe the desk but don't touch any of their fucking stuff," Andy said while dumping ashtrays of cigarette butts and roach ends. The wastebaskets were full of beer cans.

Dry camp?

He stepped over mounds of what might have been on the bed: blue jeans, magazines, sweaters, newspapers, empty chip bags. All of it clearly disgusted Andy.

"And whatever you do, don't give the men any paper towel. Tell them you've got just enough for camp," he growled. "Don't do their laundry if they ask you—you could get into big trouble for that. And don't make those beds if they leave anything on them." Then he lowered his voice. "One guy, if you can believe it, left his dirty fucking underwear on the pillow." Andy sputtered more curses and moved on to teach me how to clean the bathrooms.

"All you need is under the cupboard." He bent over his belly and pulled out Windex and Duck Toilet Bowl Cleaner. "Like this," he said and, with a Duck flourish, sprayed the toilet bowl, the shower and the sink. The brush for the toilet was in a coffee can on the floor, and the sponge mop for the shower was in a closet. "Take a used towel," he said, picking one up and using it to clean the sink and taps. "There. Make sure you refill the toilet paper, stack up fresh towels and keep an eye on the soap. And do the floors on your way out." The mirror took a quick shot of Windex. The three bathrooms had to be cleaned, top to bottom, three times a day; the ladies' bathroom, once.

Next we moved on to floors. I tried to lift the mop. It was like dragging a tree. Meanwhile, Andy filled the push barrel with a hose from the laundry taps. I watched him mix bleach with pine cleaner, his head deep in the fumes.

"Do the hallways in the afternoon when the men are sleeping, and the kitchen floor after every meal." He took the mop out of my hands and dropped it into the barrel. One section held the hot toxic bath; the other had a funnel with a lever to squeeze the mop. Andy moved a lot without moving much. I was mentally doing the math of his daily chores times 49 days. He told me to change the cardboard mats at the main entrance every day and showed me how to cut up boxes and tape them together onto the floor. Finally, I was to make sure that the men took their boots off at the door.

"I've got two mattresses because it's softer," Andy said about the bed in the camp attendant's room. I looked around my new home. Cleaning supplies and dry goods filled the cupboards and shelves along one wall—light bulbs and coveted paper towels—over stacks of quilts, blankets and pillows. On the opposite wall, beside the bed, was a narrow closet where I could stash my suitcase. In one corner, a bouquet of mops and brooms leaned over a canister vacuum. As in all the other bedrooms, there was a desk with a lamp and an alarm clock. The campie's room had the only line to the outside world, the camp radio phone.

"Don't let anyone use the phone. And don't clean the cook's room or the cook's helper's. They don't clean your room."

On the drive out, I had asked Stan who my boss was. "I am," he'd answered quickly. Andy's instructions made the campie job separate from, if not equal to, that of the kitchen staff. I couldn't imagine anyone telling Andy to do anything.

He lit a cigarette off the one still burning in his mouth and made an odd sucking nasal sound, a cavity grunt and snort. Just before we left the room, he looked me up and down with what I took to be a mixture of pity, disgust and despair. I guessed he was hoping at least one fucking roll of paper towel would survive his absence.

"Do the Rec Room first thing in the morning," Andy said next, leaving the campie's room and opening the Rec Room door.

"What time is that?" I followed his lead.

"You gotta get in and out before the dayshift crew gets up at six—empty the ashtrays and wipe the tables down. Just pick up the junk left around and empty the garbage." From somewhere on his body, Andy whipped out Windex. "Use this on the tables and the TV screen," he said and gave the air a wide spray. "Then use the wet floor mop to clean the carpet on your way out."

The Rec Room had to be vacuumed Saturday before 7:00 a.m., when nightshift came back—but not before 6:30 a.m., when dayshift was watching the news. As Andy talked, he yanked full garbage bags out of the canisters beside the door. It was time to learn garbage.

"I'll leave my coat and gloves for you to use," he said, pulling a parka from the rack by the main door.

He'll be back! All of a sudden I realized that employment with Legacy didn't mean I would stay at this camp. The thought of going to another camp was too much to absorb. So was the thought of staying here. My head was pounding from the tour and the smoke. I pulled on my cousin's boots and followed Andy out the door.

The incinerator was a few hundred yards away from the camp building. I'd never seen anything like it before: an industrial burner with a smokestack about 15 feet high. The machine was a gigantic metal box, maybe six feet high and five feet across, with a door at waist height. Stuff was sticking out of the incinerator—dials, pipes, gauges—that meant nothing to me. It was black, dirty and oily. I was afraid of it. Beside the incinerator sat a boxcar-sized steel bin for metal scraps.

"You open the door like this," Andy said, two-handing a set of heavy clamps, "and use this shovel to pick out all the metal from the last burn, the cans and lids." He dug through the ash and tossed a few crispy brown rings into the bin. Then he lifted a couple of plastic garbage bags, shoved them inside and closed the door. "Make sure the clamps are tight and then turn this dial to start the burner. Do you hear that?"

I heard a hiss.

"Turn it again when you hear that sound—okay? And make sure you take out the kitchen garbage before the bags get too heavy."

Black smoke billowed out of the stack over our heads. Of all the jobs, I thought I'd like garbage the best: fresh air.

I followed Andy back inside camp to learn how to do laundry. The dirty sheets had to be bundled in a special gunnysack every Friday morning by six for pick up by the laundry service, which dropped off clean sheets at the same time. Andy showed me how to tear off the plastic wrapping around each set of sheets so they were ready to go on the beds in a hurry. All the other camp laundry was my responsibility: kitchen and bathroom towels.

"I get the wash going first thing at five," Andy explained, "so I don't run out when nightshift comes in at seven to shower."

It was a grim image: a wet naked man reaching for an empty towel bar after a 12-hour night shift on the rig—no fucking towels!

"You've got lots of time to do your job," Andy repeated several times. "Take your time."

We had walked the hallway square again, Andy pointing out cupboards and closets where supplies were stored. Every few feet he'd check his watch and let out a grunt-snort-suck in frustration. We found Lil and Isabel in the kitchen, looking out the window.

"Watch out for Old Tom," Isabel said to me. "I had to tell him to fuck off yesterday. But once I did that, everything was fine."

"Yeah, don't worry, he's okay," Lil added. "You'll get the hang of it. Just tell him to fu—hey, truck's here!"

Andy, Isabel and Lil grabbed their bags and ran for the door—flat-out ran. I could hear the low rumble of a big engine close to the camp building. Instantly, Stan appeared and opened the back kitchen door. As soon as he did, a woman burst over the threshold, laughing loudly, slipping and catching herself on the wet floor.

"I'm Frankie," she called out in a loud voice. "I'm the new cook's helper. I just left another camp—I didn't even get to go home and Jason phoned and asked me to come here. So here I am—I didn't even get a change of clothes." She announced this as if it was a great joke. "Dammit!" Her dark brown hair swung with her laughter.

While I was standing there, dumbfounded at the sudden switch, a cardboard box flew through the air in my direction. I lunged and caught it, almost falling under its weight.

"I'm strong," Frankie proclaimed. "I've got great upper-body strength. I used to work out, you know, pump iron. These are easy for me. Here, take this," she called and heaved another box at me.

The woman had the voice to match the muscles. She was taller than I was by a few inches, maybe five foot nine, and about 175 pounds, not fat but husky, solid. And she was right—she had a good throw.

"Is this too hard for you?" Frankie laughed at my awkward catches. She had dark brown eyes, a wide smile with straight white teeth. I guessed she was in her early 40s. Her voice was strong; she didn't mind being heard. She hadn't stopped talking since she'd come through the door, moment by moment, life as it happened to her.

"And I was tryna' tell him, you know, he's not that bad looking, but he hasn't been laid . . . "

"What are all these?" I called to Stan between diving for boxes and Frankie's reflections on the sad sex life of the delivery truck driver.

" . . . the poor guy, his girlfriend broke up with him and . . ."

"It's our supplies from the grocery truck—we have to unload it," he answered over the box in his arms.

" . . . he's never gonna meet anybody. 'Look,' he says to me, 'it's Friday night and I'm sitting way the fuck out here,' and I tried to tell him that after my ex and I split up . . ."

I ducked out of Frankie's range and leaned out the back door into the dark. At first it was so black I couldn't make out what I was seeing. Then my eyes adjusted and focused on the open end of a semi-trailer filled with boxes. It was 9:00 p.m. The three of us had to unload the truck tonight. After all the trucks that had nearly blown the Toyota off the road, a semi was going to kill me after all.

" . . . the poor guy needs to get some, you know, it's not good for us to go—hey, Stan, where do you want this box—boy, this is a light one."

We threw, carried, lifted and stacked box after box: boxes full of lettuce, bacon, hams, turkeys, raisins, coconut, cake mixes. Out came four-litre bottles of pickles and mayonnaise, cases of ketchup, flats of eggs, bricks of cheese, tubs of margarine and crates of milk.

"Let me carry this," said Frankie. "I'm way stronger than you." She walked by me with a box of frozen roasts in one arm, swinging a sack of potatoes or carrots or onions with the other.

There were more bananas, apples, oranges, more loaves of bread and cans of jam than I had ever seen in my life, except maybe in Safeway, where I'd negotiated a maze of pallets to find the bathroom. It took the three of us more than an hour to unload the truck. Only later did I remember that Andy, Lil and Isabel were sitting in the cab of the truck the whole time, waiting for us to finish so they could leave.

When the last box was off, the driver pulled out. Stan and Frankie and I stood and looked at each other over leaning cardboard towers that blocked the cupboards and doorways. My back hurt. I wanted to cry. *Was this still the same day I'd left Chetwynd?*

"Go to bed," said Stan. "Go on," he waved, "get out of here—you're exhausted."

"Yeah, go to bed," said Frankie. "We can put this stuff away. Boy, I'm really tired too. I left the other camp . . . "

I hesitated.

"Go to bed," Stan ordered.

I went. Between boxes I had caught glimpses of the crew in the hallway. They seemed to be mostly younger men, darkly tattooed, with shaved heads and silver earrings. *Pirates!* Manly howls and hoots erupted from the Rec Room. The air was bloated, rancid. I kicked the wedge tight under my door, as if that would stop the seepage.

Andy's bed didn't want me on it. I pulled the charcoal blanket over my head and pressed my body against the wall. *Absorb me.* I prayed for a miracle, a molecular rearrangement, a one-time emergency transport to another reality.

I can't stay here. I could use the radio phone and call Aunty Madge. I could tell her to call Legacy and say there was a family emergency. Smoke had seared my throat and lungs. *I have to get out of here. How can I get out of here?* The skin on my back wanted to be on my front. I rolled, tossed and turned, skewered on the spit of my own bad ideas and snap decisions. *Why did I leave my car? Will they know if I use the phone?* The sheet tightened around my arms and legs. Men yelled, swore, laughed, slammed doors. The wall shook. Finally the alarm went off. What a relief. 4:00 a.m. Time to get up.

$100

"Morning, Barb—coffee's on." Stan did a quick twirl between the stove and the counter. He cut a sharp figure in his trade uniform, a double-breasted white tunic and big cook's hat. Bacon and hash browns sizzled, and on the warmer, stacks of wheat toast ripened the breakfast air. Stan was a man at home.

"Yeah, get a coffee, Barb," said Frankie. "Boy, that was some job last night, all those boxes. How many boxes did we unpack last night anyway?" She spoke with her back to me, leaning over a cutting board and a timber of cheese. "What time did we finish, Stan?"

"Smells great in here. I'll grab a cup and take it to the Rec Room," I said. It was too early to feel worse than I already did. It was time for Windex.

The Rec Room was dark and deep, almost as big as the kitchen, and windowless. I took the room in slowly, let this sanctuary talk to me about the men who played and rested in here. Two broken-down beige couches faced the big-screen television in the far left corner of the room. Beside the doorway stood two refrigerators, one filled with cans of pop, the other stuffed with raw fruit and vegetables. On the

31

right, against the wall and beside a bar sink, were eight chrome chairs and a round card table. Centered in front of the couches was a brown arborite coffee table, about six feet long and three feet wide; it looked like a coffin. Overflowing ashtrays, empty vodka bottles, half-full beer cans, gutted candy wrappers and chip bags littered the room. Nicotine, alcohol, sugar and television—the elixir of numb. The room walls were bone bare, a dry bluish grey palette. It was hard to believe the room could sustain life. Whatever had sucked the juice out of Stan and Lil and Isabel, this was its lair, the heart of the building.

I got to work. Cigarette butts fell like tiny white bones into the sand bucket. I washed the ashtrays in the bar sink; warm water livened up the acrid smell. It didn't take long to fill the garbage canisters. I tied off the full bags, picked up garbage and beer cans, turning my nose away from the yeasty stench. When the coffee table was clear, I doused it with Windex and pushed the rag against whatever had spilled and hardened. The arborite shone. Anything with a front or a top got its face washed: the TV, the card table, the refrigerators. Following Andy's instructions, I wet the mop in the laundry tub and hauled it back to the Rec Room. Then I dragged the grimy rope cords back and forth over the carpet. It was almost 5:30 a.m. I was sweating; my coffee was cold.

Frankie had already showered in the ladies' bathroom. I decided to save my own shower for later in the day and just brush my teeth and comb my hair. This was the hard part: looking at my face, those sagging eyelids and deepening wrinkles. My skin was blotchy. Drugstore dye jobs had fried my hair in uneven bars of burnt brown. It was board-straight and just long enough to pull back into a ponytail. There. Blunt bangs hung over my eyes.

No makeup. For most of my life I'd been told that my dark blue eyes were beautiful, that heads turned when I made the effort to dress up and smile. But the attention had always made me self-conscious, awkward. Friends who knew me well teased me about my flossing fetish. I'd inherited my father's strong even teeth and, generally, the balanced proportion of his German/Scandinavian features. I knew that I could look pretty, but that was not what I wanted here—not what I had wanted for a long time. Now I wanted to match the walls. Just do my job. Survive.

I noticed toothpaste drizzled on the chrome taps. *That will clean up nicely.* The kitchen garbage would be filling up by now too. I remembered Andy's warning about letting the bags get too heavy. *Get going.* The first of the morning crew was getting up for breakfast. They looked mostly in their 20s and 30s, maybe close to my son's age. I thought of the semis that had passed me on the highway—so huge that I could only take them in life-threatening pieces. The men steered around me in the same way, a fast camera-pan blur of annoyed muscle. A tattoo across a shoulder mass. A chain cabling a thick neck. A towel over a wide forearm. I was a blot, a nit in the hallway. One man glanced in my direction. No one spoke. I looked down, a mop with feet.

"Grab some breakfast," called Stan, seeing me back in the kitchen. Shania Twain sang from the safety of the radio. Three of the men were already eating at the table. Dayshift was showering, eating, watching the news, getting ready to leave for work. The same truck that brought the nightshift back to camp took the dayshift to the rig, from seven to seven, around the clock.

"No thanks, Stan, not just yet. I want to get the garbage done." The canister beside Frankie was almost full of peelings. "Wow, that's a lot of carrots. Are those for lunch?"

"These are carrot sticks for the rig boxes," Frankie said, turning to look at me through her bangs.

"What are rig boxes?" I asked, smiling, as I heaved out the full bag and tied it off. Andy had new garbage bags folded in the bottom of all the cans, making it easy to start a fresh bag.

"Those." She pointed her foot at the big Rubbermaid tote on the floor beside her. "They go out with the truck—it's their lunch," she answered. "The men really like what I give them. I put in cheese and carrot sticks, celery, you know, finger food that's really easy for them to pick up and eat with their hands."

"How do you want your eggs this morning?" Stan called out to a couple of the men as they walked into the kitchen.

"Don't the men like what I give them, Stan?" Frankie called across the floor.

"You got it," Stan sang back. "Ready for eggs yet, Barb?" He was whistling like a man who had just been laid.

"I'm just going outside to burn the garbage first." I wanted to time my own breakfast between the men's shift change.

Coats hung on pegs, and boots lined the shelves at the main door. It took a few minutes to work down the row and find my own. Finally, when I opened the door, −25 was a cold smack in the face. Nose stinging, I dragged the garbage bags across the snow, away from the lights of camp and into the dark. Carefully, I rehearsed Andy's teaching: dig out the metal from the last burn first—but it was still too dark. That would have to wait. I stuffed in the bags, locked the clamps, turned the dial; listened and turned again. *Whoomp*—the burner ignited.

Then I looked up and almost staggered. How could I have missed the stars? While the garbage burned, I gaped at the sky until my eyes stung from the cold. How had I forgotten there was such a thing as stars? When had I stopped looking up? This show went on every night while I smothered myself under pillows and bad dreams. I thought about my son, Brian, and daughter, Melissa—how much I missed them, how quickly they had grown and left home. I thought about their mother, that dour-faced woman in the bathroom mirror. What a traitor. She had wrecked my life. *I miss the woman, the mother, the someone I used to be.* Head back, I exposed my raw throat to the dark morning sky and let memory fill my starless heart.

TRIBUNE BAY, HORNBY ISLAND, JULY 1985

I spent this month's family allowance on a canvas tent and three Zellers air mattresses. Brian is five, Melissa is six and I am four months sober. It's our first camping trip, just the three of us. Their father is gone. I have a restraining order. All day we play at the beach, skim unlucky sand dollars across the blue waves, retch and laugh at the gross outhouses. In firelight, we burn marshmallows and trace the Big Dipper with smoulder-ing sticks. My children turn their apple chins upward to gaze at the starlight. Lately, I cry a lot; my infant remorse awake to what is lost and found.

I was cold; it was time to get back to work. But before I left the incinerator, I prayed. "Good morning, God. Well, here I am—the campie. Whatever happens to me now is up to you. Please keep me sober another day. Help me do the work. Keep me safe. I'm kind of an idiot. Amen."

◆

"What'll you have in your omelette?" called Stan, still at the stove. "Mushrooms, cheese, onions, ham?"

"The works," I said, smiling. The kitchen clock said 6:45 a.m. It felt like noon. Frankie was peeling and chopping potatoes.

"The cook's helper didn't do the prep work she should have done for me before she left," declared Frankie. "She should have left everything ready for this day. I shouldn't have to do all this prep—dammit!" she swore, laughing. "The cook at the last camp got me to do way more than I was supposed to do the day I left. I was doing her work too."

Frankie had a funny way of laughing at herself—hey, look at me get screwed over! Something about her body was always swinging, her clothes, bobbed hair, the axe of her jokes over her own head. She wore a loose tan-coloured shirt over black slacks. The counters were higher than standard, but she still had to bend her back over the cutting board as she worked.

Abruptly, she stopped chopping and held up her gloved hands. "I have a latex allergy," she said to Stan. "I have to go into town and see a doctor. I need cortisone cream for this rash."

While the discussion of leaving camp got underway between the two, I finished eating and left the kitchen. It was time to make the beds and clean the bathrooms before the nightshift came back.

The Derrickmen's bedroom was stifling hot and smelled like sour milk. The blankets pulled off easily; I tossed the sheets in the laundry bag. It took several attempts to get the right lift and the right amount of sheet to suck under the mattress. These weren't going to be Andy's two-minute rooms. Loose tobacco, toenail clippings, cigarette ashes, stuff spilled all over the desk between clock radios and pocket books. I knocked things over in my hurry and tried not to step on anything breakable. Empty the garbage, make the bed, wipe the counters, pick up the bags and run to the next room. *What if I'm not done before nightshift comes back?*

The Drillers' bedroom had broken blinds that gave the room a crazy wink. I tried not to look at book titles or underwear and measured my steps around the mattress, which enjoyed a few dozen bounces while I teased the sheet into place. Next door, Motormen had used both beds and gave me twice the trouble. Somebody had puked, probably into the garbage can. Leasehands ate chips in bed. My back ached from bending and pulling up the mattresses. By the fourth bed, I was sweating. *Don't look at their stuff, just keep going.* The garbage bags and laundry sack got heavier. I tried to imagine Andy doing all this work over that belly. According to Stan, the nightshift would be back about 7:30 a.m., leaving me less than 20 minutes to finish the bedrooms and clean the bathrooms.

I can't breathe.

Two bedrooms left: Roughnecks and Room 6—another bedroom I had forgotten. By now I was almost running. Every room had its own stink. Roughnecks reeked of garlic and sour socks. I had to watch my step; slippery newspapers and clothes were all over the floor. The faster I tried to make the bed, the worse it got. *I'm not going to be able to do this.* The sheets confounded me. I imagined one of the men trying to sleep on a bed coming apart, sheets all twisted, growing more furious by the minute at the idiot who had made it. Finally the sheet held in place, anchored with blankets and a pillow.

Surprise and relief. The bed in Room 6 was an ordinary mattress on a metal mesh frame. Nothing was on the floor and there was just a clock radio on the desk. I sniffed. The window was open to the mercy of outside air. Whoever this guy was, I liked him.

The bathrooms were next. I expected the worst of men in camp, so it was a surprise to find wet towels hung on the bar and toilets flushed.

As I set to spraying with Andy's flourish, I reasoned that camp life was close quarters—all the men shared the same bathrooms. What one man left behind, another walked right into. No doubt they were blunt. Nothing was anonymous; privacy was impossible. Maybe they kept each other in line.

Suddenly I remembered the laundry. *Were there enough towels?* I ran to the laundry room. Neat stacks of white towels filled the shelves. *Mercy.*

The crew cab pulled into the camp just as I walked back into the kitchen smog. The dayshift men were pulling on coats and boots. I poured myself a coffee. Stan and Frankie were talking to each other over the noise of the kitchen fans and the radio, taking a break between breakfast servings. The nightshift passed the dayshift leaving. The lineup looked like an end-of-game handshake when both teams had lost.

"What happens now, Stan?" I asked.

"Oh, the boys shower, get something to eat, relax a bit before going to bed. I'll get some shut-eye myself after lunch." He spun the tongs in the air and caught them while he talked.

Frankie turned from what looked like 30 pounds of shredded cabbage. "Yeah, I'm going to sleep this afternoon too. Barb, do you think you could bring me some extra blankets for my bed? What time did we finish unpacking last night anyways? Dammit!" She swung her hair and laughed. "I did prep at the camp I left yesterday. The woman who was relieving me sure has an easy day today. My hands feel like clubs . . ."

"Sure, I'll grab some blankets for you right now, Frankie." I escaped. The noise and smoke levels were rising. Bedroom doors slammed, and the television boomed through the Rec Room walls. Blanket in hand, I opened the door to Frankie's room. Instead of heat and stink, a blast of

engine noise hit me. Her bedroom was right beside the camp generator; the huge machine was just on the other side of the outside wall.
How can she stand it? The walls must be shaking. I would sooner sleep
in my car. Yet Frankie hadn't said a word. It didn't make sense because
she had plenty of words about everything else.

I left her room and went into the laundry room, across the hall.
Now I understood why Andy started laundry at 5:00 a.m.—the bins
of used towels from both shifts were full. I hadn't realized how
much laundry came from the kitchen. Both Frankie and Stan had
bins where they tossed dishcloths and tea towels; by now they were
full. I got the washing machine going and looked at my watch. It
was 8:00 a.m. and still dark outside—the day had not yet dawned.

My mouth was dry. The tide of smoke was rising. As I walked to
check the bathrooms, a man about my own age met me in the hallway. It was the first time I'd seen him and I was surprised: he was a
lot older than the other men, or at least looked it. His blue eyes were
red glassy balls. He swerved to pass me, lost his balance and hit the
wall with his shoulder. I gave him a brief nod as I passed. He stared
for a moment and then half fell through the Rec Room door. We were
both surprised. When he closed the door, the Rec Room let out a
boozy Friday-night belch, except it was early Wednesday morning.

Guessing the men were finished with showers, I cleaned the three
bathrooms again and multiplied the laundry. Back in the kitchen,
Frankie was standing where I'd left her, chopping, talking. Stan was
scouring the griddle and piling up pans for her to wash.

"Should I wash the floor now?" I asked.

"Yes, but wait till Frankie's finished over there—the floor's slick
when it's wet. You could take the garbage out," Stan suggested. "How's
it going Frankie? Almost done?"

"No, dammit!" Frankie laughed. "I have to get these dishes done. I don't know what's wrong with my hands—they're just not working. I'm going to catch a ride into town tonight with one of the riggies and get some cortisone cream." She held up two blue-gloved hands. "The itching is driving me crazy."

"How many men work here?" I asked Stan, who was putting the big stove to rest.

"This is a small camp. We've only got 10 on each shift, so 20 that stay here. But others guys come if they're working up here and need a bed. They stay in Room 6. Trevor's in there now. You'll see him—he drives the grader."

Ah, the fresh-air guy. I nodded.

"It just depends," Stan continued. "Some of the camps have what they call hot beds. That means one guy is getting out of the bed while another guy is getting into it." He unbuttoned his tunic and tossed another towel into the bin. "I'm going to catch a few," he said and turned on his heel.

"Me too," said Frankie. "I think I'll leave these pans to drain dry."

I gathered the garbage bags and tossed them out the back kitchen door, then went to the coat rack again and found my boots, coat, gloves and toque. It was good to get outside. The day was cloudy and had warmed up to a milder sub-zero temperature, somewhere in the mid-teens. I dawdled. Stuffed in the garbage bags. Kicked the snow. Turned the dial. Listened to the hiss and ignition of fuel. Looked at smouldering camp vents. *God, please.* My brain was numb. Beside me, the fire stammered over Frankie's wet cabbage cores. I looked up at the smoke, over the combustion of waste, and said, "You'd love it here, Dad."

The phone call: "He died."

Shock is like childbirth. The body knows what to do and takes over. Mine makes me extremely thirsty.

I carry my father's ashes to the edge of the Fraser River and tip the box quickly. I expect the wind to carry him farther away to the deeper currents. Instead, the ash drops heavily and forms a thick grey lump in a few inches of muddy water at my feet.

My father loves fire. He has fires in the backyard burn-barrel and in the basement woodstove. He has fall cleanup fires, spring pruning fires, bonfires for fun, garbage fires and funny fire stories about exploding spray cans and missing eyebrows.

For over 40 years he works as a kiln operator for a cement plant. He brings the vocabulary of heat to the kitchen table: clinker, slurry, Fahrenheit.

His daughter should know the weight of ash.

The Rec Room morning party was underway. I passed another couple of men in the hallway, but they seemed oblivious. The kitchen was empty; time to wash the floors before Stan came back to start lunch. All the chairs had to be stacked on the tables and the mats pulled up. I dragged the push barrel into the kitchen. The floor was mucky, especially around Frankie's sink. Slowly I worked down the length of the room. When I hauled the barrel and mop back to the laundry room, the washer and dryer were waiting for me.

Daylight didn't break until after 9:00 a.m. By then I had lost myself in laundry and worry. Stan hadn't said anything more about my car or any special arrangement with the Trumpeter Hotel. I was beginning to suspect he'd said the first and easiest thing that came to his mind at the time. *What if the hotel has it towed away?* Legacy was paying me $100 a day. Impound fees for the car could total my wages. I could be working here for nothing. I remembered Frankie saying she was going to hitch a ride into town—maybe I should go with her and get the car. But how would I ever find my way back in on that road?

There was a lull between meals. Stan had explained that the night-shift boys usually "relaxed" until lunchtime and then slept until dinner at 6:00 p.m. The kitchen staff caught naps between meals and shift changes. My next chore, besides laundry, was washing the kitchen floor again after lunch. Once I'd folded all the towels and stacked them on the shelves, I decided to go to my room and rest.

The radio phone tantalized me. *It's still not too late to call Aunty Madge.* Raucous calls came from the Rec Room. I'd passed another couple of men on the way to my room. They'd scowled and looked away, eyes bloodshot and hard. Even in here my lungs hurt. I noticed a vent near the ceiling that allowed air to circulate between the rooms. I climbed the shelves, stood on the counter and used a garbage bag and Andy's duct tape to seal it off. Then I cranked up the thermostat and opened the window. When I stretched out on the bed, I could feel waves of heat squandered to the incoming cold air like sin through my fingertips. *Take that.*

SURREY, BC, 1950s, '60s, '70s, '80s

He works day shift, afternoon shift, graveyards. "You have to cut out the middleman," he tells us three kids. He never misses a day of work, saves his money, avoids credit and counsels us to buy land: "They're not making any more of it." He grows our food, hunts and fishes, shuts off taps, turns off lights, lowers heat, recycles, reuses, resents. Sometimes, especially after graveyards, the kiln comes home churning inside him. He wants to leave the city and move up north. He never does. He has a good union job at a cement plant.

Soon, kitchen sounds roused me. I got up and put on another load of laundry. Back in the kitchen, a couple of the men hunched over plates of macaroni and cheese. Stan waved at me with a spoon but kept his attention on the stove.

"Hi, Barb," said Frankie. "Did you sleep?"

"No, not really," I answered, "but it was good just to get off my feet and rest. Does all this standing bother you?"

"Oh no, not in the least." Her voice rose, as if to a challenge. "I *love* my job. I just love making good things for the men to eat. I *never* get tired."

"Well, it would kill me. I just couldn't stand that long." I smiled at her and then turned to Stan. "You know, I'm kind of worried about leaving my car in that parking lot in Grande Prairie. It's only a little piss-pot, but it's all I've got left. I don't want to lose it. If it's towed, it'll cost more than it's worth to get it out. What do you think I should do?"

Stan kept stirring. "I can't have both of you gone at the same time— no way. Frankie's going to get a prescription later, right?"

"Mark's taking me . . ."

I interrupted Frankie before the talk turned away to someone else's sad sex life. "Then maybe I could go tomorrow and bring it back into camp?"

"You'll have to see who you can get a ride with," said Stan, but without much encouragement. "You could leave the car at my ex-wife's in Grande Prairie—she wouldn't mind." His voice lifted a little.

"No thanks, Stan. I'd feel better bringing the car here."

"Whatever," Stan said, "but they *really* don't like having too many vehicles here at the camp site."

The small victory felt like two warm hands resting lightly on my shoulders as I left the kitchen and walked to my room. I had risked Stan's displeasure for the relief of having the Toyota here with me in camp. It would change things. He wouldn't be my only hope. If camp life got too bad—bad enough to risk driving the Weyerhaeuser Road back out alone—I could leave.

Now what? I sat at the desk to calm down and figure out which chore to do next. All was quiet. The nightshift had finally gone to bed, most of them without eating. By the time Stan and Frankie wrapped up lunch, it would be time to haul out the garbage and wash the kitchen floor again. Then I'd do the cardboard mats and mop the hallway. Until then, I was on my own.

Stopped in those few quiet moments, I felt the nudge of an inner open hand, empty, expectant, asking for a reward. *I stood up to Stan.* The best I could offer was the luxury of a long shower. And it was there, in the pummel of hot water, that I remembered Andy, Isobel and Lil stuck waiting hours for the supply truck. Yet the camp parking lot was lined with rig workers' vehicles. It seemed only camp staff was here without transportation. Maybe that's why Stan had said "they" didn't like too many cars in camp. Too many campies would leave.

◆

Later, I washed the floor and burned the garbage. Andy had shown me how to cut and measure the cardboard doormats and tape the edges to the floor. On my hands and knees, I shifted pieces to fit together. *Cut and paste.* Each piece had to be secure so no one slipped. Snow and ice fell off boots in dark puddles that the cardboard absorbed. *I am a child on my knees.*

Next I mopped my way around the camp hallway, through the laundry room and the pantry. By late afternoon the laundry was finished. Stan and Frankie had disappeared again, I assumed to their rooms to rest. With the afternoon chores done, I tried to do the same. Daylight gave up and by 5:00 p.m. it was dark.

♦

Stan was up, twirling silver ladles like batons, and frying chicken for supper. Frankie was washing pots.

"Would you like a hand with those dishes?" I offered, uncertain what to do next.

"No way," said Frankie. "These are nothing. You go rest. I'm going with Mark into town when he gets back from the rig."

"Make sure you find your way back," Stan called to her across the noise of the fans.

I wandered to my room to read. In the rush to leave Quesnel, I'd thrown the essentials into my suitcase: the text of *Alcoholics Anonymous,* the December issue of *AA Grapevine* magazine, the Bible and, for some reason that wasn't clear to me now, a frustrating book called *How to Stop the Pain* by Dr. James B. Richards. I'd read it a few months earlier and it hadn't stopped anything.

Bedroom doors slammed. I couldn't stop myself from flinching. Volume from the Rec Room rose and fell as the door opened and closed. I rested on the bed and turned the pages of the AA magazine but couldn't absorb the words. The vinyl mattress interrupted my concentration, reminded me of the sleepless beds and colicky nights that brought me here.

VICTORIA, OCTOBER 2000

It's a furnished one-room apartment. Good thing—I've lost, given away, thrown away or sold almost everything I owned. My house is gone. Soon I'll file for bankruptcy. This old sofa bed makes a fine rack.

VICTORIA, OCTOBER 2001

I can't think; I can't work; I can't pay the rent. David and Tracy push their dining room table against the wall to make room for me. Tracy strings a sheet across the doorway for privacy. Boxes of my stuff are all over their house. When I lie on their couch, the frame presses into my spine. Under their dining room table, I can see a ridiculous box of china from my hope chest.

QUESNEL, DECEMBER 2002

Aunty Madge and Uncle Clifford in Quesnel have a solution to the problem of me. An old logger friend has a travel trailer that I can live in over the winter. It's old and small and leaks. The mattress is rotten. The furnace is broken. Aunty Madge lends me a sleeping bag good to −40 and runs an extension cord from her mobile home to a small cube heater for the trailer. The first night, I put the heater on the floor. After a few minutes I move it closer, on the counter. Then I pull it right inside the sleeping bag with me. I hope to burn up and

*go to hell in my sleep. It's −22 outside and the trailer curtains
are blowing inside. When I wake up in the morning, my hair
is frozen to the pillow.*

Soon the nightshift boys would be pulling on their boots and trading places with the dayshift boys at the door. Frankie already knew all
their names and was surprised that I didn't. Things were taking a while
to come into focus. *I don't think I can see anymore.*

Stan had explained that dinner wasn't over until the last shift had
eaten, usually by 7:30 p.m. Then I could wash the floor.

I got up and left the room to eat supper between the shift changes.
Then I cleaned the bathrooms and washed the kitchen floor for the
third time that day. Soon after, Frankie left with Mark. Stan was in the
Rec Room with the boys, as he called them. *You could go out the door
and just keep walking.* Roars from the Rec Room competed with the
pounding bass of the television. The kitchen was finally quiet; I turned
down the lights, dumped the push barrel and wrung out the mop. For
the last time I hauled the garbage bags out to the incinerator and gave
God back Wednesday, January 15, 2003, the longest day of my life.

No one saw me leave or come back inside. I wedged the Camp
Attendant door shut and rolled blankets against the gap at the bottom
of the door. The temperature was supposed to drop to −39. My window
was open and ready for it. I put on pajamas and forced in earplugs. Deaf
and mute, I rolled into the cranky bed and closed my eyes. The white
road moved through my body as I slid from consciousness to another
place that was not home.

$200

Garbage was my favourite job. It took me outside the camp, away from the smoke, the booze and the racket. I liked the plastic *shhhhh* across the snow crust, the uneven tug of the bags against my grip. It was 6:00 a.m. It could have been midnight. The camp lights barely reached the incinerator, half a schoolyard away from the building. I usually had about five bags, so it took a couple of trips from the kitchen door to the incinerator, a hulking black outline, the smokestack lost to the stars. My body was a choir: boots, breath and the work.

I turned the latch and heaved the ripe slop of garbage into the acrid black mouth. I'd already learned a couple of things. For instance, peelings didn't burn if they were all stuck together, and the boys often threw plates and utensils into the garbage. I guessed it was their compliment to the chef and the menu. Maybe the waste made them feel better, a little *fuck you*. Or maybe they just didn't want to pick up a dirty plate and carry it to the counter. Meanwhile, I burned bags of food.

There was a time when I bought expensive vitamins and mineral drinks. Every week a truck had delivered a bin of organic vegetables to my front door. The bookshelf in my kitchen back then was full of books with torn covers, pages stained from years of use: *The Art of Vegetarian Cookery, Garden Way's Red & Green Tomato Cookbook, The Moosewood Cookbook, Earl Mindell's Vitamin Bible.* I dried herbs and flowers and made crabapple jelly. "Never eat anything out of a can or a box," I was fond of saying. I figured anything white—sugar, bread, pasta or rice—was close to poison. It was too bad the memory of choice hadn't left as quickly as the money to exercise it.

The day before, I had opened a garbage bag full of bread, brand new unopened loaves.

"Could you toss this?" Stan had asked. He must have seen the look on my face. "It'll expire before the boys'll eat it—I've already got a freezer full and I need the room," he'd explained.

I had stomped over a hill, out of sight, and thrown the bread on the snow for the birds. Then I'd stood back to watch their easy feast. The ravens and crows flew over and around the scattered bread but they never touched it. I tried not to take it personally or see the frozen waste as a metaphor of my life. Maybe the birds knew better than to eat white bread.

◆

Back in the kitchen, Stan performed at the stove, a couple of fast steps and a ladle twirl to Shania Twain. He cut a dapper figure in the white tunic, almost naval. Frankie swayed at the counter, her dark hair swayed, the tan shirt and black pants swayed. I noticed she wore the same clothes she'd worn the day before.

"Good morning," they called over the blasting radio and stove fans. I asked what time they had started and then said something like "ug" at their answer.

"If you stay up and play with the boys at night, you'd better get up with the men in the morning," Stan cracked.

"Dammit," said Frankie. She laughed and pushed her hair away from her face with a gloved wrist. On the counter in front of her was an impressive heap of carrots and celery, about 20 pounds' worth. "The cook's helper didn't do the prep work she should have done for me. I did all this work for my replacement at the last camp—she would have an easy first day. Dammit, I did all the work there and now I have to do it here." She almost doubled over, knife in hand, at the funniest thing she'd heard so far.

"I'd better get going." As I left the kitchen, I heard Frankie manage between gasps of laughter, "And the cook at the last camp got me to do way more than I was supposed to. I was doing her work . . ."

Why did she keep saying the same thing over and over? Was there something wrong with her? Or was she trying to tell me something that I was supposed to know? Was she stoned or just stupid?

Meanwhile, it was time to clean. Mangled chip bags, candy wrappers and empty vodka bottles littered the Rec Room. Crushed beer cans surrounded ashtrays fist deep with ash and stubbed cigarettes. The room reeked of a place I used to live and knew I could easily inhabit again. Thirteen years since I had quit smoking, and still my body craved nicotine. In some ways it had been harder than stopping drinking. With alcohol, the cravings had come at specific times, the end of every day. I felt the urge to light up every waking minute. I could still taste the first drag, the sexy insanity of breathing hot smoke into my lungs. *Get to work.*

•

I already had a system of doing laundry and garbage around meals and shift changes. It wrapped up with my escape out the back kitchen door. When I went to get the kitchen laundry, Stan and Frankie were trading camp stories. Stan was talking about the camp in Chad. He said that Africa was great and he wanted to go back. He said you could get laid for 50 cents; for seven dollars you could have her for a month. She would stay in your room and wait for you, but you had to make sure you took her clothes when you left. She wouldn't leave without her clothes.

Frankie thought this was hilarious and reminded us that she had come to camp with only the clothes on her back. Then she turned and said to me, "Stan's number one and I'm number two. When I'm away or asleep, you're in charge."

I knew what she meant: I'm the boss of you. But I didn't care because by now I could see that Frankie was the boss of nothing. It was too bad she felt she needed to put me in my place. As far as I could tell, peeling potatoes and scrubbing toilets put us both at the bottom of the Alberta oil barrel. I decided I'd try to get on her good side anyway.

"What was that shit we were smoking last night?" she asked Stan. "My hands won't work, they feel like clubs," she said, heaving a rig box onto the floor. "The men really like what I give them," she directed to me. I didn't ask what she gave them.

Somewhere in her shadow was a place that suited me just fine.

◆

Andy was right. He'd said I would catch on fast. By midday I knew my job. It was the men I didn't know. I had to figure out who belonged to which room and when it was safe to go in and clean. Every time I opened a bedroom door, I held my breath.

"Do you want a riggie for a boyfriend?" Frankie asked.

"No. If I'm going to do that, I want to get paid for it."

This cracked her up. She'd already called me "strait-laced." Stan had sidled up to me earlier and asked, "Do you at least smoke a joint?" The kitchen staff party started after breakfast. He wanted to know if I was good for something. I shook my head for no. Stan had shrugged his shoulders and pulled a face. It was the kind of face that said *Suit yourself—loser.*

Now that nightshift had passed out and gone to bed, I decided to write a letter to a friend between loads of laundry. I wanted someone to know where I was.

Dear Marion,

Here I am, in the middle of nowhere, trees and sky as far as you can see, and nothing else. It's almost –30 outside. There's ice inside on the windows and on the inside seams that link the camp trailers. This camp is supposed to be "dry" but this is a formality—most everyone is drunk, stoned, coming down or going up. I am the "campie," the camp cleaner, the only sober . . .

I knew Marion would know what wasn't here: AA meetings. Alcoholism never took a day off, and even 17 years sober was no guarantee. That story never changed. I knew one of the main reasons people went back to drinking: they stopped going to meetings. They isolated themselves from support and found themselves in "slippery" places, where a drink and any reason met. I folded the letter and tucked it inside my Bible. It would break Marion's heart if she knew what had happened to me. I could see her holding the letter, baffled, powerless to help. How could I tell her that I had lost everything I'd worked so hard for, gone crazy with grief and good ideas on Prozac? Some letters edit themselves right out of a stamp.

♦

Frankie was right. I was a square. I worked in a square and lived a square life. The camp building felt like my body. I worked up and down the hallways but always ended up right back where I'd started. My logic hit dead ends. I didn't make sense even to myself. I thought about my family and friends and wondered if they thought about me. I tried to measure the results of prayer, to justify all the time I'd given to meetings and helping others, my belief in the rewards of sobriety and the promises of right living. *Look where you are now. Is this what my faith earned?* To think that everyone I loved might love me only as far as their front door was more than I could take. Something was wrong with me.

The truth didn't really sink in until Frankie asked me where I lived: nowhere. Stan had already warned me that a move was in the works and that I'd be expected to help pack up the camp as the trailers were dismantled. No fixed address. It would be hard to get much more shadow than that.

♦

The hallways were quiet. Frankie and Stan had disappeared from the kitchen; the Rec Room was empty. I'd never been a daytime sleeper, so I decided to go for a walk beyond the camp clearing. First, the usual chore of getting dressed. When the temperature dropped to −39, Stan had offered me his coveralls. They fit me perfectly. I pulled on cousin

Darlene's boots, my own toque and Andy's gloves. The closer I got to the door, the faster I wanted out.

The cold still shocked me. I'd lived my whole life in southern BC, where winter survival merely required all-season tires and a decent fleece jacket. Here, my Victoria winter coat would be like wearing a Kleenex. Stan's coveralls had lining so thick they almost stood up on their own. I made my way through the powdery snow across the parking lot and stopped to take in the brittle clear sky, blue against the iced white pines. Only my footsteps jarred the frozen silence. At the edge of the camp driveway I paused, looked down the road in both directions and let whim turn me right.

Of course, there wasn't much consideration given to pedestrians—it was either on the road or in the snowbank. At least in this direction I knew there would be some traffic if I ran into trouble. On the other hand, the trouble might be traffic. Drivers wouldn't be watching and probably couldn't see over a two-story, half-acre truck hood. And I wasn't so sure I wanted to be seen. Did I look like a woman? I hoped not.

Ravens circled overhead. Maybe I looked like a meal.

It wasn't long before I heard the roar of an engine. I debated climbing the embankment and hiding behind a tree. What was under the snow? It looked solid enough, but what if I slipped or fell into a hole? I decided to take my chances on the road. A fuel truck came into view and I was sure the driver would see me against the white road. He slowed. I edged as far as I could up the icy bank. A peaked cap leaned over to get a look. I gave a brief salute and kept walking. He gunned the motor and, I'm sure, got on the radio.

When the fear of being out there alone overcame the relief of being away from camp, I turned back.

My last job of the day was the kitchen floor. As I worked the mop down the length of the room, Stan spoke from behind me. I jumped.

"That's it—Frankie's out of here. Do you want her job?"

"Why? What's wrong?"

"She can't keep up. I got pots piled up, I'm waiting for her prep—I don't know what the hell she's doing over there." He pointed at her counter. "And she never shuts the fuck up—she's driving me crazy."

"Does the cook's helper job pay more?" It looked like a lot more work to me.

"You bet."

"Well . . . okay." I didn't have a good feeling about this—not for Frankie or for myself. I didn't think I could trust Stan to tell me the truth. "Are you going to tell her?" Camp was real close quarters for bad feelings.

"She's out of here at the end of the week on her break. I'll tell Legacy not to send her back."

It seemed like a safe out. Still, I wasn't so sure I wanted to work that close to Stan. But the idea of more money tantalized me. It would get me off this mop.

Then his tone changed. "You really don't know how to wash a floor, *do you*?" He sounded like a lawyer.

I didn't know what to say. I'd been washing floors for most of my life and often for a living.

He walked over and took the mop from my hand. "Here, I'll show you. It's all about leverage. Watch. You see? One hand pushes, the other pulls. That way the mop does the work—not your back." He handed me the mop and waited for a demonstration that I'd understood.

"It's just that I've never used this kind of mop before." I felt stupid, like a fake floor washer.

"I didn't think so." He turned sharply on his heel and walked out of the kitchen. The volume from the Rec Room rose and fell; he'd gone in to join the party. I guessed one way to get me to take Frankie's job was to make me feel bad about the one I had.

Finally, when the day's work ended, I barricaded myself against the smoke and racket in my room. Then I pulled out the scribbler and started another letter, this one to close friends in Victoria.

"This Friday marks three months since I left Victoria," I began and then described life with family in Quesnel. I told them that I'd written a feature article for a small magazine in Quesnel, but they only paid $250, so I'd probably lost money. I described all the newspaper jobs I had applied for, finally realizing that I couldn't compete against younger, more qualified applicants. My diploma in photojournalism was outdated; I had no experience or skill with the new digital equipment and computer programs.

"Many times during the past weeks in Quesnel I would have left town; but for a tank or two of gas, I would have. Those times, I could only sit and cry. Christmas nearly killed me, I was so homesick for Brian and Melissa, my friends and familiar places."

I thanked them for the groceries they had bought for me when I was broke in Victoria and described my diet at the tables of changing hosts: "I've been grateful to eat what was offered. When life settles down, I'll work to get back to the good foods you bought for me. All my beans are still in the jars, packed away in my uncle's basement in Quesnel."

The campie job was similar to work that I'd done before, I wrote, "except for the drugs, smoke, beer and filth—you'd hardly notice . . .

Sometimes, I am afraid. Afraid that I'll lose my sobriety, afraid I'll be smoking and doing drugs with the riggies. I need to be vigilant and keep reading my Bible and AA books. What if I'm fooling myself?"

On that question I closed the scribbler, climbed into bed, turned off the lamp and counted myself richer by $100.

$300

Dan the Driller didn't want to take me to Grande Prairie.

"Are you going into town?" I didn't wait for his answer. "Can I go with you? I'm ready right now."

"I'm going right now." He looked like a man whose mother had just asked him for a date.

It was Friday night, and my work was finished. I had changed 10 beds, scrubbed four bathrooms three times, folded laundry, washed the kitchen floor three times, the hallways twice, burned garbage and worried all day about my car. I imagined it stolen and smashed up, frozen with a cracked engine block or, even worse, towed from the Trumpeter Hotel with impound charges more than what the vehicle was worth. The Toyota was my last asset. It felt like my last friend.

It had been Stan's idea for me to hitch a ride into Grande Prairie with one of the boys so I could get the car and drive it back to camp. But since Frankie's trip to town with Mark, Stan had turned sour. He wouldn't put in a good word for me. I'd need a miracle. So it was no surprise that none of the boys I asked was going anywhere this Friday night, until I met Dan in the hallway, showered and shaved, coat and keys in hand. I stood in his way and asked as nicely as I could. What a moment. He couldn't decide which one of us to hate more: me for asking or himself for saying okay.

I ran for my coat and car keys, and seconds later, when I got back, he was gone. His roommate, also a Dan, walked by me fast and dodged my look.

"Hey, are you going into town with Dan?" I called.

He snarled without breaking his stride to the door. I chased him. He led me straight to Dan, already warming up his truck. I thanked God for young men who couldn't say "aw fuck" to my face. Dan opened the door for Dan, and I climbed into the back seat. They had almost got away.

The truck was a spanking new four-by-four diesel club-cab with plush seats, broad dash aglow with gauges. We flew out of the parking lot and slammed into the black night on the white road, past turns, splits, doglegs and forks that vanished into the frozen wilderness. Once or twice, Dan slowed at a junction, hesitated at the wheel. He said a wrong turn had cost him some time on the last trip. I asked how he knew the way to Grande Prairie; I was trying to memorize his quick turns in reverse. He didn't answer. How would I ever find my way back?

The two Dans kept their faces forward and the stereo cranked. Then it hit me. They were trying not to get attached. Never name the farm animals. God, I was so stupid. The getaway wasn't the problem; the ride into town wasn't the problem. They'd have to dump me off at the Trumpeter and not look back. They'd have to go get pissed and laid and have a great time and not think about the new campie lost on the road in the dark at −29.

It just hadn't occurred to me. I'd been so worried about losing the car, I hadn't thought about the drive back. I almost felt sorry for the Dans. After all, they worked hard and this was their Friday night. I wished I could tell them not to feel bad, that I was just glad for the ride. I could have told them that I knew exactly what they thought of me because there was a time when I would have thought the same thing. Sometimes it amused me, in a sick kind of way, to realize that I'd become exactly the kind of person I had despised. Frankie had called me "strait-laced." It broke my heart. I hated the image of those stiff-necked sober killjoys, those hand-wringing, tight-kneed, joyless, brown-pump Christians and their endless potlucks. I watched the truck hood eat up the road and wished I could tell them that it was too bad they didn't know me before I got sober. Then I wouldn't be worried about how to get back to camp. I'd be loaded in their laps, earning my fare. But those nights never ended well either. Lost was lost.

We drove on. They ignored me. Their words to one another were brief, punctuated by thumb points this way or that. I searched for landmarks, anything at all in the endless trees that would give me a clue. We passed one other camp site, and farther along I saw the red tower lights of a triple rig. That was it.

The Toyota had been in the Trumpeter parking lot—if it was still there at all—in temperatures 20 to 40 degrees below freezing.

"I hope my car starts."

"Where's your car at?"

"The parking lot of the Trumpeter Hotel. Do you know where that is? I hope the car is still there."

The two Dans said something to each other that I couldn't hear over the stereo. Neither of them looked back at me. They seemed like nice guys.

I gave up on the mental map, overwhelmed by the snarled maze of unmarked turns. The road finally T-boned with Highway 43 and Dan turned left. What could I tell myself on the way back? What could I memorize now that would help me then? I saw myself paralyzed at a starburst junction, unable to decide which road to take, driving for hours and kilometres in the wrong direction until the Toyota ran out of gas. I had clocked the time at about an hour and 38 minutes from camp to the highway. Why didn't I think of asking Dan to note the mileage? Hopeless. *Just remember it's a long way.* That was the crumb I saved for myself.

The lights of Grande Prairie appeared in the distance.

"About an hour," Dan answered before I asked.

We ran into fog. It filled the gullies, a solid grey mass. Dan drove blind. No one spoke. A semi-trailer snugged up behind us, but even its lights bounced back off the fog and snow. For about 32 kilometres we dipped in and out of fog as the road rose and fell. Suddenly we were clear and on a flat runway stretch into town. A couple of lights, a couple of turns and there was the Trumpeter parking lot. It was full.

"It's a red Toyota," I said, craning to look over the rows of trucks.

The two Dans were silent while the truck tires crunched over deep icy ruts, testosterone chewing its knuckles. My heart was pounding in my throat.

"There it is!" I yelled. The Toyota was a lump under snow, faintly pink.

Dan swung the truck alongside my car. They couldn't let me out fast enough.

"I hope it starts." First I had to dig through the snow and find the door handle. Dan leaned out the window and watched. The car door opened like a freezer lid. The seat cracked under my weight. *Dear God.* I put the key in the ignition and turned it over. The Toyota started. I looked up at Dan. He gave a quick wave and, without a smile, gunned the truck. They left.

I got to work, knocking snow and ice off the car with my arms and body. The Toyota reminded me of those toy cars in the mall that cost a buck for a kid's ride. It bounced and rocked. The motor sounded like it was grinding rocks. Uncle Clifford in Quesnel had warned me not to blast a frozen windshield with hot air, to let everything warm up slowly together.

A piece of paper was stuck under the wiper blade. Carefully, I peeled it off, dreading a fine. It was a 36-hour notice of impound for an abandoned vehicle. The time was up. I wiped the car down in awe, with a swell of gratitude for the designer, for the manufacturer, for the entire country of Japan. A letter, a testimony, a salutation began to form in my thoughts. Not all the slogans and songs composed by the priests of advertising would ever come close to the sound of the Toyota's motor that night, salvation in my ears.

Finally, the car seemed ready and warm enough to leave. I slid the transmission into drive. *Clunk*. The Toyota lurched forward. The tires were frozen. The car crabbed across the ruts toward the first gas station I saw. After the fill-up, the attendant drew directions to the nearest grocery, Save-On-Foods, on a piece of paper. He didn't want me to get lost. When I turned in the parking lot, I saw that all the other cars and trucks had block heaters plugged in to electrical outlets. Once again, the Toyota was on its own.

I walked into the store, shy of its size and bright lights, self-conscious about my dirty coat and boots, the ratty brown ponytail. It didn't help that I'd just used my body to clean off the car. There had been no time to change my sweats before leaving camp, and I'd been up for work since 4:30 that morning. At my age, 48, the hours showed in dark lines under my eyes and the deep frown-crease between my eyebrows. I wasn't a small woman, five feet six inches tall and close to 150 pounds. The invisibility some middle-aged women feared, I wanted. It felt safe. But after only a few days in camp, I felt like an outlander. *Already?*

The phones, I needed to find the phones. I had to tell somebody where I was—at Trinidad 11, wherever that was . . . and in case I disappeared. A clerk let me use the store phone with a calling card, maybe because of the way I looked: stunned. Debra in Victoria answered my call. "Thank God. You're alive," she said. "We were going to send money to bring you home." *Bring me home to what?* Still, it was a nice thing to say. I said that I was fine.

Then I walked up and down the aisles, agog, uncertain of what to buy. It had been a long time since I'd been in a grocery store with more than 20 dollars to spend. Water, buy bottles of water. Nachos. Potato chips. M&Ms. The really big bag. I kept checking my watch. It was my best guess that if I left by 10:00 p.m., I'd make it back to camp by midnight.

Earlier in the day, Stan had said, "If you're not back by midnight, I'll drive up and down the roads until I find you." He had said it a couple of times, but I figured, since he was high, he just liked the heroic sound of it. Still, he was one person on earth who knew where I was supposed to be by tomorrow morning, who might tell somebody if I never arrived.

◆

Grande Prairie lights disappeared as I followed the highway south. The booty was open on the passenger seat, and I chomped chocolate and nachos together between slugs of delicious bottled water. Stuff your face, I told myself. Not only was this my supper, it could be my last.

The car radio was too feeble to hold a signal, and the speakers kept cutting out. I wished for dash lights and wedged the flashlight between my legs so I could see the speedometer. Ice thickened on the inside window glass beyond the heater's power and limited my vision. I talked to myself. *Just remember it's a long way.*

I was afraid of the gullies and hills. The Toyota was such a small car, and its lights were so dim, that if I slowed or spun out, a semi could easily smash into me. I'd be wrapped around an axle or wedged between the wheels. Or pushed over the edge. I was afraid of bones poking through my skin, of hanging upside down in the car and taking hours to die. At every corner I expected to hit the wall of fog. Small patches drifted across the highway, but as the kilometres passed it seemed the fog had cleared. I kept checking my watch, angling the flashlight at my wrist, to glimpse the end of the hour that should put me at the Weyerhaeuser Road turnoff.

There it was, the unruly roadside crop of flags and markers, the trade insignia of rigs and camps. I slowed the car to make the turn and then gunned it to make the first steep climb off the highway and into the wilderness.

My eyes stung. Oncoming lights crested the hill. I edged the Toyota over as far as I dared without going off the road. I could hear the engine roar, and when it levelled out and came head-on, the lights blinded me. For a split second I didn't know whether to hit the gas, the brakes, or the ditch, but whatever it was, truck or de Havilland, it also swerved to miss me. Heart pounding, I imagined curses in the cab as it roared by.

There wasn't another car on the road. Only a couple of trucks had passed me on the highway. The sky was clear, the snow dry, hard packed, rough. The drumming of the tires filled my ears. I stuck to the most heavily travelled ruts, ignored dark gaps between the dense trees that opened to other roads. Finally I saw the red lights of the triple rig, but they were on the wrong side of the road. Could I have missed a second rig? Easily. Another well-travelled road turned off in that direction. Would this turn put the rig on the right side? I had to let the car slow gradually so as not to spin out on the ice. Then I backed up to the turnoff and sat there in the middle of the road, idling in neutral, wondering which way to go. Well. Here at last was my life's predicament, visible in a form I could see.

Help. I imagined God climbing forward between the seats, lifting a knee over the emergency brake and sitting Himself down on my nachos. We considered the fork in the road. We got out of the car and examined the tire tracks. I shone the flashlight over the area, the black road edges in both directions, all sides, looking for directional flags. I looked up. Nothing. Soundless. Just trees, snow, sky and stars. And those red lights.

◆

There was something dreadful and deeply familiar about this place. I'd stood alone at night on roads like this before. How many times? I remembered how, at 17, I'd get drunk and hitchhike along Southwest Marine Drive for no reason at all. In those days, huge maples shadowed the road, bordered only by fields ploughed to the banks of the Fraser River. I'd dared my life to a pair of brake lights and not known why. Once I hopped into a car with a young man and his buddy and went back to their basement suite. "This one kisses funny," he'd said.

I remembered night skies over the Cleveland Dam in North Vancouver, how I'd left a carload of drunken friends and walked for an hour into the forest, thoughtless of anything other than being alone. When my friends finally found me, they were crying and furious. I'd felt nothing. Or how, as a child, night after night, I'd sneak outside after everyone had gone to sleep, to wander under the trees in the dark, terrified of being both found and lost. Why did I do it?

Maybe that's what God was nudging me toward while I searched for signs with a flashlight. *Why are you here?* But I kept pushing back, unwilling or unable to face more than the surface of things. *Which way do I go?* I'd pushed that question right to bankruptcy and, now, to the edge of my life. To my way of thinking, it had always been the same: choices I never wanted to make on roads that I was forced to drive. Except now the metaphor was real. I was alone with myself, stripped of distractions, with no way out.

I got back in the car, put it in drive and did not make the turn. I don't know why. There was no sign. We just drove on.

•

It might have been 20 minutes before I saw the lights of the second camp. Over and over I checked my watch, knowing that if I wasn't pulling into camp after somewhere near an hour and 38 minutes, I was lost. A least a dozen times I prayed and then guessed which way to go. Another intersection, a rat's nest of roads, some of them well used, others with only a single track or two in the snow. I forced myself to drive on and ignore the gnawing anguish of second thoughts. "We're going this way," I told God. He was quiet, an impassive space between black vinyl and frosty glass.

Dan hadn't stopped at junctions, and I wasn't sure how much time I'd added to the clock. Some of the camp markers were knocked over or hidden by other signs. My knees almost buckled when I finally recognized the Trinidad flag tangled in the mix. I took the turn. Down the hill, left at the next road and there it was, Mars Base II. I was already imagining how I would retell the story of the drive from Grande Prairie to camp. *I could have cried.* The lights, the generator, I rumbled into their arms and parked the Toyota between the trucks. For a few minutes I just sat there.

Then I gathered up the remains of my feast, got out and stood beside the car, not sure if my legs would hold me. Before I walked up the stairs, I looked back at the Toyota. It was just a car getting cold.

As I came through the door, Stan popped out of the Rec Room, eyes red-rimmed and glassy. He looked surprised.

"You made it."

$400

"Any morning sober is a good morning," my sponsor, Marguerite, used to say. Through two closed doors and earplugs, I could hear Stan smashing pans onto the grill. I rolled out of the noisy bed and pulled on my sexless fleece packaging: a pair of bluish grey sweatpants and matching sweatshirt. Head to toe, my body was a flat palette against twinkling rows of Windex and the curvy Duck Toilet Bowl Cleaner. I looked at Marguerite's picture on the shelf in my closet. It was a black-and-white photograph that I'd printed in my darkroom when I still had the house. The backlight had deepened the tones of her black hair, the heavy folds of her eyelids, darkened the moustache that had defied even laser treatment. I stared into her eyes. She had gazed right down the barrel of that camera lens straight into my heart. She was beautiful.

I won't drink today.

The promise gave me a place to hang the purpose of one more day. All night I had argued with vague dream shapes and now I was exhausted. "Nobody's ever died from a sleepless night," Marguerite used to say.

I sat on the bed and opened *Twenty-Four Hours a Day*, the Hazelden book that I read every morning. Today's reading began: "The new life can't be built in a day . . . " I was 46 days away from 18 years sober.

After the reading, I closed my eyes and tried to focus my prayer. "Dear God, thank you for keeping me alive. Please help me to stay sober today . . . "

Maybe it was time to get that Rec Room cleaned. Maybe Stan was wondering when I was going to show up. I struggled to find the right words to move God. *Please don't leave me here, why didn't you stop me from wrecking my life, it would be so easy to drink, why didn't you help me, I don't know who I am anymore, dear God are you fucking deaf?*

I said those bad words silently to myself for the sake of Marguerite, who sponsored me for 15 years, who died at 32 years sober. She told me not to say "fuck," because when we got sober, we cleaned up our mouths as well as our lives. But on this side of Pine Pass, it was my favourite word.

I opened the door to face campie's day.

◆

Frankie was in her usual place at the kitchen counter, in the same black pants and tan shirt, chopping the same orange mountain of carrots and cheese. She called "Good morning" over her shoulder. It sure didn't sound like it. Stan used a ladle to salute in my direction and then turned back to the spitting eggs and bacon.

What? No jig this morning?

The long double sinks beside Frankie were full of dirty pans. They looked like scuttled battleships. She had pulled over one of the garbage cans for peelings, but she had a bad aim. The rig boxes were open on the floor beside her, still empty. There was water slopped on the floor all around her feet.

I wondered if this morning's tension had something to do with sex. Maybe Frankie had spurned Stan in favour of someone else. It wasn't hard to imagine her making that choice. Was this his payback? She was falling behind Stan's breakfast pans and she had to pack those rig boxes with lunches before 7:00 a.m. Even through the suffocating greasy heat, I could feel their back-to-back posture curse the air between them.

"Barb, could I get you to keep an eye on the coffee?"

Stan's voice startled me. I was pouring a cup for myself and planning a fast exit. "Um, sure." Was he being sarcastic? I looked over at Frankie for help. *Chop, chop, chop.* She didn't look up. I glanced at the coffee machine. It was a two-pot beast. This wasn't my job. "Um, how does it work?" This was Frankie's job.

Stan flipped his flipper in the air and then onto the counter. He crossed the floor, taking exaggerated steps around Frankie's puddles. "I'll show you, and then do you want to grab a mop for this mess before someone slips and falls?"

"Oh sure." I looked at the clock. Nightshift would soon be on its way back to camp.

"You keep this pot full of water," Stan said, "and the coffee goes in here." He demonstrated the set-up and showed me the supply cupboard. "Make sure that a fresh pot is ready to go for the guys whenever they come in," he explained and snapped the filter into place. "It's the same machine in every café," he said.

Stan had a neat trick of saying one thing while his tone of voice said something else. He did his signature pivot and went back to the grill. That was another neat move.

I nodded at his back and went for the mop. It was all about leverage: he was going to use me to push Frankie.

◆

After I cleaned the Rec Room and the bathrooms, I started on the bedrooms. In the Roughnecks' room, Dave had left a pile of clothes on his bed. Andy's words were still fresh: "First, you yank everything off the bed. But if he's left anything on it, any fucking clothes, leave it. Don't make it. They fucking know better." Stuff left on the bed slowed down the campie's work.

I stood there, baffled by this rule-breaker. Should I move his clothes? What kind of trouble could I get into? Maybe there was a reason Dave didn't want his bed made. Maybe this was a test. Maybe they'd all start leaving their clothes on their beds.

Dayshift was up for breakfast and nightshift was on its way back from the rig. I had to be out of those rooms in less than 20 minutes. It was time for an executive campie decision. The clothes went on the floor in a heap with the bedding. I shook a clean sheet across the mattress, and after seven or eight tries I finally got the right sheet-sucking action and made the fucking bed.

I picked up beer cans, booze bottles, chip bags, candy wrappers, ashes and butts. Sweat puddled between my breasts and soaked my bra. My body movement created tornados of dust, skin cells and hair filaments in the air. "But don't touch any of their fucking stuff." Andy's words sputtered in my brain while I sucked foot rot and fart molecules up my nose.

Hurry. I knocked on the Leasehands' door, took a breath and barged in. By now I knew that Herb and Mark shared this room and that the Leasehand job was what it sounded like: least hand. These guys were the rig gofers.

Mark was the guy Frankie had left camp with to go into Grande Prairie. While I dumped the ashtrays and stepped over duffle bags, I wondered if that had something to do with the trouble between Frankie and Stan this morning. Was Stan jealous? Was Frankie sleeping with both of them? All of them? I remembered that when I'd asked Frankie to tell me the riggies' names, she had said that she could go for Mark but there was "that age thing." I guessed she meant the thing about being nearly twice his age. Mark looked like most of the riggies in their 20s, with silver earrings and steel-blue tattoos cabled around his arms. But to me, he didn't look dark haired and dreamy eyed—just muscles and mad. When I was burning the garbage, I'd seen him climb onto the camp roof to catch a signal for his cellphone. His rage had carried over the ice: "fuck this" and "fuck her." All I wanted to do was stay out of his way.

Ditched behind the garbage bin, the fenders of a smashed-up car poked through the snow. "Bad business," Andy had muttered. Something about a booze-up, a fist fight and keep your mouth shut, nobody's saying anything. I thought I'd heard Andy say the car was Mark's, but Blake was the one with the purple cheek and black eye. I might have made the car Mark's because it looked like him: trouble handsome couldn't hide.

I turned to make Herb's bed. He was married, in his late 30s, a Christian who bore the cross of camp with a perpetual scowl. Herb taxied the boys back and forth to the rig in the crew cab. He was homely, a short man with an odd slouch. His gnarly hair was too long and fell over thick eyeglasses. A greasy film on the lenses denied his fellow man the least of charities: mutual vision. I saw him always alone, eating in the kitchen or watching television in the Rec Room at odd hours. Twice, I had barrelled into the room and jumped out of my skin when something moved against the wall—Herb. One morning he was watching a religious program, the volume cranked right up. He didn't flinch. I fled.

I yanked the sheets off his bed. A pair of underwear lay across the pillow. "It'll take more than that, Herb." I grabbed them bare-handed and hung them on a chair. Then I pulled off the pillow. There it was, gleaming gold and burgundy, the Holy Bible. Herb was hiding a Bible under his dirty ginch. No doubt there was a special camp treatment for Bible reading, and I didn't want any part of it. After I changed the sheets, I put the Bible back under the pillow and his underwear back on top. Then I emptied his garbage, wiped up the tobacco and left the room. *Hurry up.*

Later, I found Herb in the Rec Room, smouldering behind his spattered eyeglasses. I sat down at the table. He ignored me. I said something like, "It sure is cold here." Was he smoking two cigarettes at the same time? He ignored me. I kept at it, dropping small stones of chit-chat onto the back of a sleeping bear, and when he didn't leave the room or tell me to fuck off, I asked how long he'd been at Trinidad 11.

Slowly, he turned his head to face me. "I'm here to make enough money to pay off our house. My wife hates it when I'm away in camp, she hates being alone, but we've got a five-year plan." He named a small town in southern Alberta where they lived. "I should only have to do another two years or *mumble mumble.*" He turned his head so I couldn't even read his lips. "*Mumble mumble* the five-year plan." Then his thumb hit the television remote and the volume shot up.

The door banged open and a couple of the nightshifters came in and started yelling at one another over the television.

I aimed my mouth at Herb's hairy earhole. "I made your bed today."

One more time, his head swivelled and I looked through the smeary light reflected on his eyeglasses. He may have blinked. Maybe twice for "Fuck you." Then he turned away. I got up. "God bless," I said, the best rebuke I could think of at the time.

♦

After lunch, it was naptime. The nightshift had finally passed out.

"When I'm asleep, you're in charge," Frankie said, just in case I forgot she was my boss.

"Well, I won't be here," I answered. "I've got to get out and get some exercise. And some fresh air."

"Aren't you glad we don't smoke? Don't you think it's funny we're the only two in camp that don't smoke?" Frankie peeled off her rubber gloves. It was just after noon. She was getting ready to leave the counter she'd stood at since 4:00 a.m. "I'm so glad I don't smoke—I don't even want to smoke. In the last camp I worked at, everybody smoked in the kitchen except me."

"Are you going for a 10-mile run?" Stan asked, straight-faced.

"No. I'm going for a walk." It was somewhere between −20 and −30.

"Well don't get lost—you did pretty good last night," said Stan.

"Yes, it was . . . " I searched for the words to describe the drive.

"You know, I was surprised to see you came back. After you left, I checked your room to see if your suitcase was still there."

"That's not my style. I wouldn't do that."

"Well, I've seen it before, especially with new people like you." Stan grinned and tossed his tunic into the laundry bin. He left the kitchen on Frankie's heels. Things seemed to have warmed up between them.

I could believe that someone would consider escape from camp worth the loss of a suitcase. What I didn't want to believe was that no one would have looked for me. It had never occurred to me that I could have kept driving and never come back. Or even that I could have stayed the night, paid for a hotel room and waited for daylight before attempting the drive back to camp. All I wanted was to get my car and keep my job.

The hallways were quiet. I worked my way through the layers of gear anchored on the hooks at the back door until I found Stan's coveralls. After about 15 minutes of wrestling with zippers and cuffs, gloves and boots, I was sweating and ready to dive out the door.

The blue sky was wide open, a borderless abandon of space. What a contrast to trim Victoria skies that were seldom clear of contrails, those lacy vapour lines that fenced horizons and established tidy boundaries of vision. As happy as I was to be outside the walls of camp, something about the vacancy overhead felt random, almost dangerous. In spite of the heavy crush of my boots in the snow, I crossed the parking lot with the feeling that at any second the laws of gravity would cease and I'd fly off the earth. The road parted the white sea of trees in front of me. I turned left on a breeze, away from the relentless drone of the generator, anxious to make the most of my temporary silent parole.

What would Marguerite say if she could see me now? I knew exactly what she would say. One more time, she would tell me the story of her and Mel's bankruptcy in the early '80s. She would describe how they found just the right benched property in Grand Forks and how hard they worked to build their dream home. "We dug the foundation by hand ourselves with a shovel and a wheelbarrow," she'd say, her voice full of pride, and I'd wait for her thick eyebrows to arch at the end of this sentence, the way they always did. She would tell me again how interest rates shot up and caught them with too much credit card debt just when Mel's mechanic business slowed down. She never cursed anyone, not the banks who foreclosed, not even the bailiff who'd checked their truck, nicknamed Old Betsy, to make sure they didn't leave the property with more than $4,000 in tangible assets. One more time, she would tell me how they arrived penniless in the Comox Valley, her, Mel and their young daughter Grace, and how the Salvation Army gave them coupons for boots and blankets.

At some point I'd usually interrupt to change the topic back to me and the more important problem of how I was going to make the mortgage payments, put gas in the car, and feed the kids and myself until the next court date for child support. Marguerite would listen, cigarette fixed at her lip, dark brown eyes squinting through the smoke.

"You know," she'd always say next, "the poorest we ever were was that first winter we rented a cabin down at Kye Bay—when Gracie broke her piggy bank open so I could buy cigarettes." Here she would stop, always unable to speak for a moment. I'd drum my inner fingers, impatient. I knew what came next. "We were never so close as a family as we were then." Then she'd take a deep drag and look me right in the eyes while the smoke curled out her nose and through the black curls that hung on her forehead.

I'd never known what to say. Some part of me knew that she was telling me something that I didn't want to hear: money isn't the most important thing in life. In frustration, I'd press on with my litany of worries. Marguerite would pour herself another black coffee, light another cigarette and listen as if she had all the time in the world. And when I'd run out of steam, she'd say, "Is that all? What else is bothering you?" There was always something else.

One day she had handed me a piece of paper and said, "Here. Memorize this." She'd written out a poem that her sponsor, Grace, had given to her in the early days of sobriety.

> *If you don't know what's important*
> *Then everything is important*
> *If everything is important*
> *Then you try to do everything*
> *If you are attempting to do everything*
> *Then people will expect you to do everything*
> *And in trying to please everyone*
> *You don't have time to find out*
> *What's important*

I remembered reading the poem for the first time. When I reached the last line, I'd turned the tables and quizzed Marguerite. "Who wrote this?" I asked, almost certain she wouldn't know the poet's name. She didn't, and to my reasoning this evened the score because I didn't know what was important.

Time had slowed in camp, wrenched the natural rhythms of the body to the 12-hour shift and stripped away distractions. I had time to think, whether I liked it or not: What was important? *Go back.* I'd walked farther from camp than I'd meant to and now turned around. One foot in front of the other, I tromped through the snow while Marguerite talked to me about how to get through another day sober when you've really fucked up your life.

$500

The alarm went off, but I couldn't get my eyes to open. My hand found the clock. *Not again*—another night of dreams about my ex-husband—*you're crazy.* I stretched my body to bring it back to the present. It had been 18 years since our marriage ended. The mattress cackled. It was *not* a matrimonial bed with brass hearts and the queen-sized acreage of a pillow-top mattress. How many people had slept in this bunk? Did anyone ever clean these mattresses?

Stan and Frankie's morning banter seeped through the door with the smell of coffee and bacon. It was time to start the day, but first I had to remind myself: I ended the marriage because he hit the kids and me. Some part of me didn't get it. The nightmare scenario never varied from a theme—I pleaded for his love and he rejected me. Why didn't I ever dream about his hand swinging for my face? Why didn't I dream the truth?

◆

Dr. Penny Hobson-Underwood, Psychologist

She sits on the sofa, one leg crossed over the other. Her black ankle socks have orange and yellow parrots on them. I'm here to talk about some of the odd things that have been happening to me lately. She listens while I describe the violent turn of dreams I keep having about my former husband. I also tell her about the "bad pictures" that pop into my mind. She asks what I see. "My hands cut up." She diagnoses me with depression and suggests that I make an informed decision about Prozac before I refuse to take it. Then she says, "Those are not dreams, *Barbara. Those are* nightmares." *For some reason, I can't stop looking at those parrots, the agreeable bird that just repeats what it hears.*

◆

There wasn't much of a Sunday morning Rec Room party—I guessed the boys were still suffering from Saturday night by the looks of all the horizontal booze bottles and crushed beer cans. Outside, the temperature had warmed up and softened the snow, making it harder to drag the garbage bags to the incinerator. It was already my second trip. The sky was lightening as I followed the path of my own footprints. This time I saw something new: animal tracks alongside my own. They looked like cat tracks. Fresh cat tracks. In an instant, it made sense. Every day I'd slathered a carcass of garbage across the snow. Even on my walks away from the camp, I'd assumed that everything, rodents and predators alike, was either frozen or hibernating.

I looked over my shoulder. The animal, if it was a cougar, could be anywhere; I wouldn't see it until it jumped on my back. Or it could tuck in behind the incinerator and wait for the next delivery of fresh meat on foot. No one would hear me call for help over the generator, the radio, the television, the drug-sopped indifference that made camp life bearable. Oh well. I'd given my life to God that morning. A not-so-difficult exercise when I'd already lost everything that I'd cared about, at least in terms of a cash surrender value. Nice gift.

Yet every now and again, when I thought about all the things I'd lost, a strange feeling came over me. Disconnected. Loose. Light. It was an unfamiliar sensation—almost joy. I shoved the garbage into the burner and fired it up. *Does any of this mean more than it is?* What if every time I hauled out the garbage was a chance to consider what *I* thought a woman's body was worth—no real estate or retail wealth attached? Since I couldn't figure out my rate of pay, I simply divided $100 by 24 hours and concluded my hourly value rang up at little more than four dollars. But was that the measure of my worth? It seemed so. It sure felt like it. Was that how I judged someone else's worth to me? Marguerite's worth? I thought about Stan's year at camp in Africa and some poor naked woman waiting for him to come back with her clothes, and for 30 days to pass, because he'd bought her for seven bucks.

I decided to get back inside, maybe ask one of the boys if they'd seen anything lurking around the camp. But just then, company did arrive. A couple of pickup trucks and what looked like a gas truck pulled into camp, so I finished the garbage and went back inside to see what was going on. Whoever it was had brought along a border collie. The dog drew me like a magnet.

VICTORIA, 1998, 1999, 2000

Melissa and Brian leave home for university. The vacancy is unbearable. I move into the basement suite and rent the upstairs

of the house to friends. Then my cat of 18 years dies. Upstairs,
the tenant's dog is walking around, a shepherd malamute named
Max. The sound gets on my nerves so I bring him downstairs for
company until his family comes home. He gobbles down the meals
I cook him, belches, farts and falls asleep in front of the TV—how
could I not fall in love? Soon, cancer takes him. When I leave the
clinic, the parking lot staggers with loss.

Big man voices mixed with Frankie's laughter. I slipped into the kitchen on the pretext of getting a coffee and sidled up to Stan at the stove.

"Who are these guys?" I asked.

"That's Pete. He's the Tool Push, and the others are a couple of the engineers. That's Morgan at the end of the table. He drives the water truck."

"What's a push?"

"The push is the guy in charge—Pete's the boss. Come on and meet him."

Before I could say "no thanks," Stan had tossed his ladle on the counter and walked over to the table where the new men were sitting. *Rats.* I preferred the sidelines before sticking out my neck. Too late.

"Hey, Pete—this is our new campie, Barb."

Pete paused, fork suspended. He turned to look at me. A chunk of Stan's cherry pie bled through the silver tines onto his plate.

"Hi." I put on my best "I'm a nice idiot" smile.

"Hi." The pie dripped. He glared directly at me.

Stan told me the names of the engineers, but I barely heard. Pete the Tool Push had rattled me.

"Hi," said the engineers as they nodded over their pie plates.

"And this is Morgan. He brings the water out to camp every week," said Stan.

"No Andy?" asked Morgan, the water truck driver.

"Oh, I'm his relief." I spoke quickly before Stan jumped in to say I'd taken Andy's job. Maybe these guys were his buddies. Maybe Andy gave Morgan all the fucking paper towel he wanted and let Pete use the radio phone. It had been a long time since a man had looked at me with that much disgust—18 years, in fact. What had I done? Maybe I had misread him. I didn't know how things worked out here. Maybe the Tool Push was supposed to hate everybody, especially campies. Even with a mouthful of cherry pie.

I tried another approach. "That's a beautiful dog you've got there—what's its name?"

"His name is Jake." He leaned over and scratched Jake's head. The dog never moved from his side. Pete looked up from the dog; his eyes met mine. No mistake—he scowled. I flushed.

These were big men, six foot plus, whose wide bodies carried solid muscle and forearms thicker than my thighs, whose rig work and 12-hour shifts demanded strength and endurance. Meeting them in the camp hallways intimidated me, especially when they were pissed off and drunk. But no one, until Pete, had focused that anger directly at me. He was bigger than all the other men I'd seen, in his mid-40s, with tousled curls of sandy-blond hair that fell into baby-blue eyes. His flannel shirt was open at the neck; thick chest hair popped out of the triangle. I noticed his hands around the fork: he had knuckles an octave wide. And for whatever reason, he didn't like the sight of me. It didn't make any sense.

"I hear you went into town the other night, Barb." Frankie leaned against the counter, looked at me and then looked at Pete. "What time did you get back?"

"Around 12." I started to feel uneasy. The engineers leaned over their plates, eyebrows raised.

"You drove back all by yourself?"

"Yup." I sipped my coffee and looked at the kitchen door. What was she getting at? The attention was making me nervous. I had wanted to ask Pete if I could take Jake outside and throw a stick around.

"Wow. I'd never do that. You're brave."

I looked carefully at Frankie's face. Her tone was even enough, and she was smiling. If it was sarcasm, it was good, Stan style. Had I underestimated her?

"No. I'm not brave." *Nothing to look at here, folks.*

"Stan, these gloves are way better, my hands are really healing up. I..."

Her sentence ended when I closed the kitchen door behind me.

◆

Now what? I looked around my room. Pete and the engineers had thrown the routine off. Stan and Frankie should be leaving the kitchen for their naptime smoke-up with the nightshift boys. Then I'd wash the kitchen floor and clear out for my walk. I didn't think I should leave camp—I didn't like the idea of Pete finding me alone on the road—but I didn't know what to do instead.

Had I done something wrong? It couldn't be my work. If anything, I did it too well. Sometimes I wondered what other campies did with all the extra time. No, Pete's dislike could only be caused by one of two reasons: either I wasn't doing something that I was supposed to do . . . or someone had complained about me. About what? I decided to ask Stan later.

Meanwhile, as much as I wanted to get outside, I decided it wasn't worth the risk. What protection was there for women out here? If what Stan said was true, that companies didn't like too many vehicles at camp, how could a woman leave if things got bad? What if I was threatened . . . or raped? Who'd believe me? Or find me, for that matter? I couldn't even tell anyone where I was . . . somewhere in the trees south of Grande Prairie. Whatever support I had would have to come from Legacy, my employer.

Meanwhile, I was stuck. Television was out of the question. The Rec Room, sanctuary for the men, stank. Read? I'd packed in such a hurry there'd been no time to mull over books. As well, it had been a matter of space and weight. I'd packed the way people do under orders for evacuation: triage. Instead of bandages and water, I had my textbook, *Alcoholics Anonymous*, the Bible and the irritating *How to Stop the Pain*. The books were wedged between sweatpants, gloves, flannel pajamas and a box of earplugs. What a sight. If a person's sanctuary said a lot about them, what about their suitcase? By the looks of it, I'd say whoever packed this suitcase was going to be the loneliest campie in northern Alberta.

Bible reading in daylight was too risky. The last time I read the pain book, its suggestions had just made me mad. Didn't I already have enough to feel bad about? Why did I bring it? It must have been the cover, the promise of relief. Now it was this or nothing.

I angled the door shut for privacy, but ajar enough to hear the men's voices from the kitchen. Propped with pillows, I fanned through the pages. The introduction was already marked from my last reading: "But it is easy for us to justify all manner of self-destructive behavior simply by the fact that we have been offended."

Once, I had thrown a Bible as hard as I could at a wall across the room. This book was making my hands twitch in the same way. Smoke seeped into the room; my eyes and throat were starting to burn. It was too much. The bare walls looked back at me. The room felt like a cell. I thought about my daughter and son. My throat tightened, pain collected into a big ball in my chest, tried to come up my throat like a fist. *No.* They wouldn't catch me crying—it would be almost worse than Bible reading.

I jumped off the bed and left the room in search of something dirty to make clean.

◆

Finally the kitchen was quiet; Pete the Tool Push had left with the engineers. The camp had water for another week. Nightshift had gone to bed. I lifted the mop from the steaming barrel and slopped it on the yellow linoleum. *One hand pushes, the other hand pulls.* Stan was right. It was all about producing more energy with less effort. The mop engaged the whole body, it was a working dance, and I found a rhythm to the drag of the long cords. Soon, I daydreamed, half hypnotized: saw strands of kelp roll in the tide, Morgan Freeman mop the floor as God, the hair of the woman who washed the feet of Christ with her tears. What happened after she got up and went home? I felt more like Snow White, boss of the mop and slop at a grumpy turnstile of dwarfed men.

That was not the fairy tale I'd read to my children. I didn't want my daughter led into the forest, having bitten that charmed apple, unable or unwilling to wake up and take responsibility for her life. I didn't want my son belittled by a job he hated, the magic of life sucked out of him by debt. So far, their success was the joy that made my own failures bearable. No, Snow White was my fairy tale, and Stan was the huntsman who had taught me how to use a mop.

And so the afternoon passed, almost timeless.

•

"Have you got a boyfriend, Barb?" Frankie wanted to know what the deal was with me.

It was suppertime. I was at loose ends for something to do until the next round of bathrooms and found myself loitering in the kitchen. Stan and Frankie were talking about their exes.

"I did, but I just broke up with him," I lied. It had been about a year since we had broken up.

"Aw, that's too bad," said Frankie.

"No. Not really. He was a heroin addict." That was the truth. I was showing off.

"Whoa, that's tough," Stan called over the fans.

"Yeah, it was. But heroin wasn't going to let him go—so I had to."

"What else you gonna do?" said Stan. "When my ex and I split, I told her, 'You can have either all the furniture or the condo.'" He laughed. "I knew she'd go for the furniture. What's she gonna do with no TV? Sit on a box and look at the wall?" He snorted and laughed again, taking a deep satisfied drag off his smoke.

I was thinking about the collateral value of a sofa versus a condo and how it was too bad Stan's ex didn't get some good legal advice.

"We were together for six years, and then I caught her fooling around with one of my buddies." He stood over spitting pork chops on the grill and shook his head. "And I left my first wife to be with her! Go figure."

"When I left my ex, I never took a thing." Frankie's voice was full of pride. "I didn't want to be one of those women that clean a guy out. We had a condo and everything."

Stan saluted in approval.

"Did you have any kids?" I asked Frankie.

"Yeah, I've got a son. He came with me when I left. He's 25 now—he's doing great. He's already got his own place." Frankie was swaying to the radio, facing the wall and talking over sinks full of dirty pots and pans. "Now I've got a roommate. I share a condo with him. We really get along good together."

I didn't mention my own divorce settlement. My ex had signed over the house in trade for arrears child support and future payments. I considered the real estate a better deal but it was too complicated to explain without saying more than I wanted Stan and Frankie to know. I was already "straight-laced." What would I be for "cleaning out" my ex? Pete's scowl was still fresh in my mind.

Frankie was still talking. ". . . and now I just got the settlement from the divorce. I've got 20 thousand in the bank. That's my share of the condo." She paused, took a step back, wiped her bangs out of her eyes and looked at me. "The campie in the last camp was really nice to me. He showed me the ropes and spent a lot of time talking to me about how camp worked. He was a really great guy—so friendly. Now I know everything about the campie's job."

The kitchen was heating up, the air thick with cooking fumes. It was nearing six: time for the men on night shift to come in and seethe over their dinner plates. My hair was wet with sweat, and Frankie was giving me a headache. I hadn't seen him do it, but I suspected Stan was also inching up the volume of the achy-breaky radio tunes to drown out the fans and Frankie's chatter. All of a sudden I could hardly breathe.

"Think I'll go check on the laundry" was my best excuse to escape the kitchen.

But I didn't know what I was going to do—there was nothing until after the shift change, when I could clean the bathrooms again.

I checked the washer and dryer, looked at tubs of peanut butter in the pantry, tidied stacks of towels. I wandered the hallways until I noticed the interior trailer seams: beige vinyl flaps about a foot wide, which overlapped and snapped together. Even with the inside temperature at 70 plus, ribbons of ice layered the vinyl edges around the buttons. For a while I amused myself by picking off the ice. Then I remembered that Andy had told me not to forget to wipe down the ice so the floors didn't get wet and rot around the seams. I had forgotten. Suddenly, Dan the Driller walked around the corner, bare-chested and blind, his eyeglasses steamed up from the shower. I flattened against the wall, and after he passed I scurried back to the man-less safety of my room.

That book? Or walk out the door and . . . what? Disappear into the night? *Get me out* . . . But I couldn't get out. The Toyota was a frozen lump of car-shaped snow. I got up, sat down and got up again. I walked from the bed to the desk to the shelf and back to the bed. It wasn't far. About six feet. *Something, I need something . . . something now.*

That book. I pulled it out of the suitcase and skimmed the chapters for the fast version of *How to Stop the Pain*. James B. Richards said the same things kept happening in my life, with the same kinds of people, because of my perceptions. *Oh, fuck off.* "Your mind selectively processes information . . . while ignoring data that is contrary to your point of view."

Richards said repentance was a "change of mind" that would let me see "a lot of hurtful events differently." Apparently my problems were the result of self-centred judgment and a distorted view of the world. And when I had been hurting badly enough, long enough, I might be willing to stop blaming God and everyone else for my mistakes and pain. He said that some people kept making "the same mistakes until they suffer personal destruction."

As I read those words, I felt that rush through my legs and arms again, the urgent order to get out, get away, do something, anything— *go, go, go*. My chest tightened. I looked up through the window blinds. *Prison bars*. Outside my door, nightshift was getting ready to leave. "Hey, will you pass . . . here's your . . . " The clunks and thuds of dropped boots and bumped walls; while I was coming apart, the men were gearing up for work.

I had nothing to hold me together. No car, phone, computer, candy, chips, chocolate. No friends, family, meetings, church, shopping. None of the ways and means to escape what Richards was writing about: the truth about my feelings and judgments of other people. I turned back to the book. Pain was an inevitable, but "torment was optional." In order to have a better future, I had to be free from the past. Change was up to me.

Solution? "Today may be the day you need to sit down alone . . ." Dayshift clomped up the stairs, nightshift slammed out. " . . . and release someone in the past from your judgment." Richards suggested writing a letter to each person. "It is not for the other person; it is for you." The letter was supposed to explain what happened, how it had affected me and, specifically, the judgments or resentments I had formed regarding that person and myself. Then I was to write out exactly how I "released" that person.

It was like finding the keys I'd been tearing the house apart looking for . . . in my pocket. Laugh or cry? Richards had just prescribed the AA Fourth Step.

An old friend in the program used to say that everyone at some point in sobriety "would stand alone naked in the garden with God." She'd meant to describe an intimate reckoning with God. How lovely. I had imagined a garden paradise gilded by moonlight, birdsong, the trill of water over round stones. There, God and I would stroll, arm in arm, my bare body at ease, and speak of the heart's deep mysteries.

I put down the book. Suddenly I saw the big picture: the camp, the clearing, the trees. It hit me. This was my garden. I was alone in the wilderness, stripped of my stuff, naked. It took a few minutes to absorb. *This is as garden as God gets.* Now I knew that my life depended on writing those letters, no matter what else happened in camp. It was the reason I was here. What happened after didn't matter. I looked around—cleaning supplies, light bulbs, blankets—the ordinary articles of life. Some temple. Camp was the end of the line, the end of who I used to be or thought I might become. I had nothing left to go back to and no way to go forward. It all made perfect sense. How else would a person end up naked in a garden with God? From the outside, nothing appeared to change. I sat perfectly still. On the inside, the ice began to fall off my seams.

◆

Pork chops and applesauce, mashed potatoes and gravy, pudding for dessert: what a feast. After supper I worked my way through three bathrooms and washed the kitchen floor for the last time that day. Stan and Frankie had joined the Rec Room party. Doors slammed like gunshots, the throbbing volume of hoots and hollers rose with heat and smoke levels. As soon as I finished the chores, I sealed myself off in the campie's room with my scribbler at the desk.

The first letter I wanted to write was to Melissa and Brian. They'd heard the news of my bankruptcy second-hand. I couldn't remember the last time the three of us had been together for a heart-to-heart. How much did they know or understand about what had happened?

Melissa was 24, Brian, 22; I'd raised them on my own since they were six and four years old. It had always been just the three of us.

For the past two years I'd been too self-absorbed and then too ashamed to face them. What must they think of me now?

When I got sober in 1985, my sponsor, Marguerite, gave me a plaque: "There is no higher calling in life than raising the children God has entrusted to your care." I had centered it at eye level on the shelf over the kitchen sink, and it had stayed there for years. Those words had grown into my soul and shaped the purpose of every struggle, every day. I put my dreams of a university degree and a career as a writer on hold. I made a decision to stay single, to give everything I had to make a better home life for them. It was my choice; there was only so much time and money. I kept pushing back what I wanted for myself because I wanted their success more than my own. But when they left home, those delayed dreams rushed into the vacuum and overwhelmed me.

I picked up the pen. As I wrote, I tried to imagine how Brian might feel about my not seeing him before I left for Quesnel. I wondered if he knew where I was now. I thought about Melissa studying for exams and facing pressures I knew nothing about. What did she know except that there was no home to go back to if she needed it? I could see that, like alcohol, the means I'd used to escape pain had only increased it.

Dear Melissa and Brian,

I'm so sorry. When you both left home for university, I went a little crazy. The silence from your empty bedrooms was louder than anything I was prepared for or would have believed. It overcame me.

You are the joy of my life—I'm so proud of the adults you've become and of what you have achieved. It's been hard to let go—I'm so grateful for the purpose your lives gave mine and how your needs defined my own. I wish I could say that there weren't days when I felt sorry for myself and resented how hard things were sometimes. Try to imagine how it felt to be on my own for the first time in my life. I had the diploma and a great idea for a book. But I lost my way. My thinking was confused and I made wrong decisions to fix bad ideas.

Although I still don't understand why I did some of the things I did, it's more important now that you both know how much I love you and miss you. Every morning under the stars, I close my eyes and see your faces. Then I ask for God's protection and blessing over your lives.

Please know that all the time it might have looked like I had forgotten about you, because I didn't phone or come over, because I moved other people into the house and into my life, I was only running from the unbearable pain of missing you. Please forgive me for not facing my pain and, more importantly, for not coming over to see you and talk about what was happening to all of us. I release you from any guilt about decisions I made. I love you.

GOOSE SPIT, COMOX, 1986

Melissa and Brian play in the waves at the ocean's edge. I sit on a blanket, lean against a log and watch them. There's no money for camera film. Take a picture with your mind. Brian digs into the sand with his toes; Melissa taps the water with a stick. A gust of wind catches their hair. Fine strands of yellow fix memory to this wealth.

$600

It was time to learn how to talk with the boys. I let my arms hang loose and faked a confident stroll into the Rec Room. Good, just Trevor and Eric, smoking and watching the news before supper. The rest were either in the showers or still in their bedrooms. Even better, these two seemed to have a lower rage level. It probably helped that they smoked dope like tobacco. One of the couches was empty. I let myself drop heavily onto the cushions, the way confident people do.

One day in the kitchen, Frankie had told me that she had eyes for Eric too. He was a Motorman, shiny shaved head, ripped body. He took a deep sexy drag, and when he leaned over the ashtray, he glanced up through thick eyelashes that framed those dark brown eyes and smiled at me. I must have smiled too.

"Hi."

"Hi."

Trevor from Room 6 sprawled at the other end of the couch, one leg anchored on the coffee table. An arm dangled a cigarette close to one of the cushions. I already knew that Trevor wasn't a regular part of the camp but a special driver hired to operate heavy equipment like tractors and front-end loaders. He had different hours than the rest of the crew, depending on when and where they needed him and on what machine. Trevor was the only one who opened his bedroom window, and he always had a hardcover book on his bed. And while probably close in age to Eric, early 30s, Trevor hadn't shaved his head, pierced his ears or decorated his arms with skulls and snakes. He had a lanky, less muscular build, pleasant features, and a more mature, almost preppy, style. I'd noticed that he wore shirts instead of T-shirts, and slacks rather than blue jeans or sweats. Of all the boys in camp, Trevor scared me the least. Right after Eric, he said the next polite thing.

"Hi."

"Hi."

We all watched the television together. It felt almost normal. Practically family. I tried to relax and listen to the news. It was hard to pay attention because my body and my brain started an argument. Urgent messages poured in from various organs. Generally, they said, "Get the hell out of here." My arms and legs said they didn't know what to do or where to go. They demanded new orders that didn't make them look stupid. "Uncross us. Fold us together. Keep us apart." My heart intercepted their frantic messages and started to pound. "I'm letting go," warned the bladder. *I'm staying put.*

And then a commercial break.

"This is the first camp I've ever been to," I said to the couch with men on it.

"Really?" answered Eric.

"Yes. I'm from Victoria—I've never seen anything like this," my arms flailed widely, "before in my life."

Both Trevor and Eric nodded.

"Have you been down to see the rig yet?" asked Eric.

"No, I haven't had a chance, but I'd like to see it."

"You should get Pete to take you down there," said Trevor.

"Umm, yeah, that'd be great. I don't even know what a rig does."

Eric launched into an intelligent and detailed description of how an oil rig worked. Over the static in my ears from my organs and extremities, I read his lips and caught references to "drill, water, casing," but missed the important words that described what went down and what came up.

". . . and so that's why when something goes wrong, it *really* goes wrong—hard and fast. Because everything operates under such extreme amounts of pressure and force, if . . . breaks and somebody's in the way, it's usually fatal."

"Did you hear about those two guys that got killed a couple of weeks ago?" asked Trevor.

"Yeah," said Eric.

The two men continued their discussion about the accident at another rig. Their vocabulary quickly lost me. Meanwhile, the racket inside me had quieted, diverted by normal conversation. Now I began to feel strange in another way. Even my sweatpants looked odd and out of place, more like a goofy costume than regular work clothes. I squirmed. Something was wrong. Until now, most of the boys had been a vague raucous mass that moved through camp at regular intervals. They had been drunken howls behind a barricaded door, a tattooed blur of ashtrays and empties that I picked up after. I'd come into the room expecting . . . what? Not this. I felt more foolish by the minute.

Eric and Trevor continued to talk. The news was still on television, but the real news was that there might be something askew with how I saw men. Maybe my decision to stay single for the kids had been noble. But now I wondered if it had also been a decision to stay afraid of men. For the first time I understood what Richards meant when he said my perceptions determined my judgments. The idea that my judgments about the men in camp were suspect made my head feel like it was going to split in half. I had believed that I was trapped with a gang of violent drunks. What if I was wrong? What if they were exhausted boys with too much money and not enough common sense about booze and drugs?

I sat on the couch and tried to imagine a man looking down the hallway at the campie's door, shut tight. From here, it looked at least anti-social. He wouldn't know that the campie was afraid of her taste in men. He wouldn't know . . . what I didn't know.

"I guess Tom had a rough shift," Trevor said and laughed.

The talk turned in a direction I could understand. "Which Tom?" I asked. There were two Toms in camp—"Old Tom" in the Derrickmen's room and "Young Tom," the other Motorman, who shared the room with Eric. At first I guessed they were talking about Old Tom, because he was staggering drunk whenever I saw him. Even from a distance, I'd heard the boys making jokes about him. Old Tom was the camp drunk.

"Eric's roommate," said Trevor.

"Oh—not Old Tom?"

"No. Young Tom." Trevor laughed again. "He went into town last night and had to take a taxi back to camp. Made it just in time for work this morning. Guess he had quite the night."

Eric snorted and laughed. "His truck's still in Grande Prairie?"

"He took a cab from Grande Prairie?" I tried to guess at the mileage in dollars . . . probably over $200.

"Yeah. Herb said Tom told him it was a $1,300 night. And he still has to get his truck back."

Both Trevor and Eric guffawed while I marvelled and did the math—13 days of my wages on a one-night drunk. I wondered how much these guys were earning that made $1,300 funny.

"What'll he have to do today? I mean, what exactly does a Motorman do?"

"He takes care of anything with a motor—it's an important job on the rig," said Trevor.

"That's what I do," said Eric. "I make sure the pumps, hydraulics, whatever—that all the machinery is in good shape. If . . . "

"When," Trevor interjected.

"Yeah, *when* anything mechanical breaks down," said Eric, "I fix it. It's an important job. Rig time is money."

The Rec Room door swung open, and Blake walked in. When he yanked on the fridge door, I could see from the light that the bruises on his face were fading. Still, he looked rough: pale, with scraggy blond hair to his shoulders, and always in the same red-and-black-checked flannel shirt. He shared the Derrickmen's room with Old Tom.

"Well, I'd better get going," I said, and with a quick nod toward Trevor and Eric, I paraded my baggy-pantsed self out of the Rec Room.

◆

It was snowing and dark outside. I'd made the usual rounds and now hauled the garbage out to burn. Under the angled floodlights, the air shimmied, iced with crystal flakes. Farther away, where the light fell off, glazed trees edged the clearing at their roots. Beside me, the mechanics of the incinerator made hot music to chicken parts and potato skins. My eyes gradually adjusted to the deeper shades of snow. The night felt familiar to my interior landscape; when I drew in a sharp breath, my teeth hurt. A person wouldn't last long out here.

MOKA HOUSE ON COOK STREET, VICTORIA, DECEMBER 2002

"I've got a solid gold tooth—see?" John pulls his mouth open with his finger. I don't want to look. His teeth are really bad. "Monica paid for it," he says. Monica is the woman before me. "I'm saving it. I can't believe it's lasted this long already." I know what he means: that he hasn't had the gold pulled to cash in for heroin—yet. "What do you think it's worth?" he asks. This conversation must be a dream. I can't be here with this man.

I spoke. "Thank you, God. Thank you for the gift of sobriety today and for keeping me safe."

My words dropped to my feet like little stones. No. Those words were for the Sunday pew, the obligatory parrot words. What prayer fit here? I turned my face to the sky and felt the snow on my face. A real prayer would erupt from the gut and rip through the chest. It would push that fist of pain through my throat and I'd scream into God's dark ear.

However.

A scream didn't seem like a practical idea, although it probably wouldn't have mattered. I heard the sound of a truck coming down the road and guessed it was Herb bringing dayshift back from the rig.

"I'm going to write a letter to John tonight."

I listened: the crackle of fire, the wind, the generator, the truck motor getting louder. "Good night, God." I scuffed my way through the weightless snow and clomped up the stairs. By the time I'd pulled off my boots and Stan's coveralls, Herb the Christian was at the door.

•

"Gonna grab a plate, Barb?"

"Sure, thanks, Stan."

"Whoa, look at your face—it's all red," said Frankie. She'd turned from the sinks to see me.

I put my cold hands to my burning cheeks. "Yeah, I guess I was outside longer than I thought. It must have been the wind."

"The cold doesn't bother me at all. I'm used to it," said Frankie, and then she turned to Stan. "My son and his buddies all have snowmobiles—we all go out . . . "

Frankie's words were lost to the general racket as I turned my attention to my belly and the warming trays. It was a small thing, but I loved the surprise of lifting the lids to discover what Stan had prepared. Tonight it was meat loaf and mashed potatoes, carrots and mushroom gravy. Every meal was a secret celebration; I never yelled "Wow—look at all the free food!" but I really wanted to. What a giddy freedom to heap my plate, knowing there would always be more. My vegetarian diet had disappeared the first day in camp. *She doesn't drink, smoke, screw . . . or eat meat?* It would have been safer to read the Bible in the Rec Room than to ask for a tofu burger in the kitchen. I wished I could eat alone in my room. But there was a rule that plates had to stay in the kitchen; otherwise there would have been food slopped all over the camp. So I ate at one of the tables in front of Stan and Frankie and whoever else showed up. My heap of mashed potatoes looked like a mini Pine Pass; it made me self-conscious. I angled my left arm in front of my plate and ate as fast as I could.

•

"I need you to fill out this card for our records," the woman says. She looks tired. This isn't my first time in a food bank. But it's been about 16 years since the last time, when the kids were little. Now it's just me. She takes the card when I'm finished and puts a coloured sticker on the corner. "You can come once a month," she says. "Any time—but only once a month." She points to the counter where I will get in line for my ration. "It's usually better at the beginning, " she adds.

Debra gives me a ride home. There's no gas in my car. On the floor beside me is a plastic bag of groceries. I'm numb. Later, I set the items on the counter, one by one. Nothing is whole except cans that can't be opened. Everything else is a part of, a piece of, separated, chopped up and divvied out. One quartered margarine. A half loaf of bread. A baggy of break-fast cereal. Crackers, one cellophane row. A couple of dry soup mixes. It was all No-Name–brand products, the cheapest of the cheap. This wouldn't feed anyone more than a few days. It was chemical-laden processed crap. I was ashamed I had taken it from someone who had to eat this shit to stay alive. I threw most of it into the garbage. If this was the better beginning, I was really fucked. The fridge was empty.

◆

It was Monday night, a week since I'd left Quesnel. Andy would have been proud of my beds; I could get the bottom sheet tucked under the mattress in one fast flip. After the rooms, I finished the day navigating around the dayshift's 15th hour. As soon as I turned off the kitchen lights, I closed the campie's door and pulled out my scribbler.

Before I started John's letter, I reminded myself of the goal—to acknowledge what happened, to admit how it affected me and, finally, to forgive.

Dear John,

I can't say that you robbed me. But all my money is gone. You never asked me to buy you heroin. Not once. "I can play you like a fiddle," you said later. How can I say that I was robbed? When I was insane with grief, crazy on Prozac, you came over to my apartment for coffee and never went home. Do you remember the morning I left hospice? You were waiting at the door. "Marguerite died," I said. "How do you feel?" you asked. I remember trying to feel something, anything.

I told you my secrets. That I'd waited for God to bring me a husband. That I was afraid that I might pick another wife-beater and that I'd been scared celibate for years. You said that it was God's joke on me that it turned out to be you.

You only asked me to do one thing. "Save me," you said. "I'm going to die."

Now I know why you made up your needles and left them on the desk beside my computer. If I stuck one in my arm, you could say that I never asked you to give it to me.

Just so we're clear, I ended our "friendship." I brought your stuff to your Frances Street squat and took back my car and the keys to my apartment. A couple of weeks later, I saw you at our regular coffee shop. I knew, after living with you, that there are no chance meetings or coincidences, that with heroin, every single minute of the day matters.

You said that when you went back to heroin, after 16 years of sobriety, that you honestly believed that you would die. But you didn't.

Did I save you? You said I did.

Did you save me? You distracted me from the stash of T3s and that big bottle of Percocet hidden in the closet.

You needed heroin and I came along. Though I'd like to believe there were times when you fought with your conscience and you wrestled the drug that wanted to own me too. Or maybe you knew that, like all the other women, I'd leave you behind soon enough.

You were a gift and a crime. Thank you for being on the floor beside my bed when I woke up in the night. Thank you for being there in the morning, for needing heroin and, therefore, needing me. Thank you for being a problem, a presence, a conversation, a dilemma, a heartbreak in the room with me. You may have saved my life. I forgive you.

$700

Tuesday: sunny and −30. I fell into the mindless routine of bathrooms, floors, laundry and beds. It was like meditation in a saloon, the hum of ashtrays and empties. Apart from kitchen interludes with Stan and Frankie, I moved from room to room without speaking.

I worried. I wanted to make sense of where I was and how I'd got there. I tried to apply the logic of my work to the events of my past. Why couldn't my life make as much sense as cleaning a bathroom? Shower first, sink second, toilet third, floor last. Start from the top and work your way down. Bring the dirt and germs to the bucket on the floor. You wouldn't have to clean the same thing twice; you wouldn't drag toilet germs onto the sink. Then you could stand back and see the results of your hard work. If I could see where I went wrong, maybe I wouldn't have to keep cleaning bathrooms—or, as Richards said in his book, keep making the same mistakes "until personal destruction."

I remembered when I'd graduated from the Western Academy of Photography, the awards I'd won in photojournalism. Student loans and credit cards, a tenant in the basement suite, by hook or by crook

I'd made the mortgage payments and supported the three of us. When the 10-month program finished in the spring of 1996, I'd had a plan to write a book about spiritual retreats on Vancouver Island. I thought about the trips to retreats, the interviews and photography. All supported by credit and the false cheer of Prozac. How did I think I was ever going to pay that money back? Did I even care? With each wipe along the rim, one more time, for the thousandth time, I tried to explain to myself why I was here now.

◆

Loss occurred. Dad died of cancer in 1997. Both kids left home in 1998. The cat died, the dog died. And then menopause: sleeplessness and sweat. I broke my ankle and needed two surgeries. I couldn't run. It was a warning—*stop!* Because I'd worked for years as a bank loans officer and knew how to fill out credit applications, I mortgaged and re-mortgaged the house. I knew that a clear-title house outweighed vague statements of purpose and no proof of income. I knew what bankers wanted to believe. Years of resentment and restraint hijacked a $75,000 line of credit. The first week on Prozac, I treated myself to $1,000 on face makeup. After three years on Prozac, I couldn't make tears.

I lied. I refused to admit that I was spending out of control and tried to buy peace with my past and myself. Instead of selling a publisher on the retreat book idea, I sold it to myself. Instead of establishing a foundation of writing and research, the retreats became personal interludes where I photographed icons and took long garden walks.

I daydreamed. I talked to Marguerite in a vague and defensive way about my book plans. She was angry because she had seen how hard I had worked all those years raising the kids alone. "You're going to mortgage that house right out from underneath you," she'd snapped. She was the only one who said it to my face. And that's exactly what I did. But not before I'd phoned my mother and glibly asked her to lend me $35,000 to travel across Canada. The publisher I'd contacted had expressed interest but said the market was too narrow. However, national coverage might interest them. Beyond all reason, all sanity, the cross-Canada flight of fancy possessed me.

I blamed. The memory of that phone call was excruciating. It wasn't my mother's immediate and common-sense refusal, or that I had exposed the lunacy of my behaviour to my family. I could only imagine the kitchen-table discussions in my absence: *What's the matter with her?* The same question had tormented me: Why hadn't anyone come over to see what the hell was the matter with me before it was too late?

Bad blood. Something was wrong with my expectations. I knew that now. Love had limits and I had surpassed mine. Because I had come so close to it myself, I now understood how people found themselves living on the street. If they had family and friends, they probably had worn them out over the years, exhausted the muscle of love by borrowing money and breaking promises. Depression and grief—those twin hosannas of potentially bad ideas and dumb moves—had turned me into someone even I didn't know.

Bad bets. When credit couldn't pay credit anymore, I panicked. When, after months of waiting, the publisher said, "No thanks," I realized that no one, including God, was going to rescue me. I could "name it and claim it" until kingdom come, but there would be no retreat book. It was a mistake to mortgage the house and it was another mistake to sell it. In October 2000, the real estate agent brought the first and only offer in six months to the Victoria hospice. I signed the papers in the rooftop garden and went back downstairs to sit beside Marguerite's deathbed. Later that day, I couldn't remember what the offer had been, but I thought it might have been close to what I'd paid for the house 10 years earlier. Six months later, May 2001, I filed for bankruptcy. After a couple of subsistence jobs, I was on my way to Quesnel to live with my uncle and aunt while I got back on my feet. It seemed like such a good idea.

No doubt there were other reasons, financial and hormonal influences that I'd failed to acknowledge. How honest could I be with myself? It was like doing my own root canal. But at least if I owned the obvious mistakes, there was hope I'd learn the lessons from them. I reminded myself of all the places in Quesnel where I'd applied for work—not one response to over 20 applications. Not even from the Billy Barker Casino Hotel, where I'd dreaded a yes. No, I left Quesnel for the same reason I'd left Victoria: because I was utterly demoralized and flat broke.

Maybe it was the shock of all the times I'd moved—I had to keep telling myself how I ended up here. Still, the chorus: *why didn't you . . . you could have . . . what are you . . . how could you . . . loser . . .* the kind of lyrics a drink would shut up. Sobriety wasn't supposed to be like this. My life wasn't supposed to be like this. *Poor me, poor me, pour me another one . . .*

◆

I couldn't feel my nose. It was too cold to go for a walk or linger around the garbage. Back inside camp, it was naptime; the Rec Room was quiet. I pulled off Stan's coveralls. A clatter of metal broke the silence. I dropped my boots and pushed open the kitchen door to see if Stan or Frankie had fallen. Nope, it was Frankie at the sink. She was alone.

"Hi, Frankie. Sorry, I didn't mean to scare you—I thought . . . "

"Were you outside?" She leaned over the sink, a collision of dirty pots and pans all around her. "I'm getting these pans caught up. Boy, that Stan—he can sure use up the dishes—dammit!" She laughed like a mother indulging her little boy. "I'm going to take a break after this."

"Can I give you a hand with these? I'm all caught up for now." I picked up a dishtowel and spoke again quickly, to cut off her refusal. "Yes, I was burning the garbage. It's so beautiful outside. I've never seen country like this before . . . have you?" By now I had a cooking sheet, one end balanced on the counter and the other on my forearm. The pans were heavy, huge, almost two feet by three, and hard to scour. I wondered to myself why Stan didn't cover the pans with tinfoil to bake on—it would have saved a lot of elbow grease and sweat over the sink. Considering all the food I threw away, it couldn't be the budget.

"Oh yeah, I've seen lots of this country—it's beautiful." She glanced over her shoulder at the window and then looked at me through her bangs, her brown eyes beautiful and serious. "You don't have to do this, you know. I can manage. Stan's making a big dinner tonight and he needs these pans this afternoon. I'm going to get ahead of him yet!"

"I know." I shrugged my shoulders. "It's no big deal." It was though, the first time we'd talked to each other without Stan in the kitchen. I grabbed another pan and smiled. "So what did you do before this? Have you worked in camps before?"

Frankie pushed her hair with a gloved hand and straightened her back. "No way! The last camp was my first—I loved it there. Before that I worked in lots of different jobs, you know, hospitality." She watched me dry the pan. "What about you, what did you do?"

"Oh, same thing, different jobs, whatever I had to do—cleaned houses, sold furniture, and just before I came here I worked at a bed and breakfast for heart patients. The job was like what I'm doing now—cleaning bathrooms and doing up rooms." I laughed. "But heart patients are a lot quieter than this."

Frankie grinned. "The boys need their relaxation. They work really hard—it's good for them to let off steam." She added another couple of pots to the stack in front of me. "You can leave these to air-dry, you know."

"Yeah, I'll just get these big pans out of your way." Counter space was opening up. Frankie drained the sink and refilled it with clean water. For a while we worked side by side without speaking. The radio was off, the exhaust fans silent. Sunlight brightened the kitchen. Water slurped and pots clunked. I hoped for a space to open between us that didn't include Stan, and I wondered what he had told her about me. Frankie and I probably weren't going to be buddies, since our ways parted at the Rec Room door, but still . . .

"That's enough for now. I'm done." Frankie smiled and snapped off her gloves. "Thanks, Barb."

I draped the towel over a bar. "No problem—I had the time."

Frankie stepped around the puddles, gave a wave and left the kitchen. Now I could wash the floor.

•

My chores were done. I decided to write the next letter, to my ex-husband, and rehearsed the purpose. What happened? How did it affect me? How was I going to release and forgive? I looked at the blank page in the scribbler. I thought about my marriage. I remembered that line from *Jaws*: "You're going to need a bigger page."

Dear Ron,

What happened was that you hit me. I made excuses for you and blamed myself. I hated you for destroying any hope of trust. What happened was that you lied and said it never happened. Or if it did, that I deserved it. That I provoked you—anybody would have reacted the way you did—that if you behaved badly, well, that was my fault too. You blamed me. And I blamed you. And caught in the middle, Brian and Melissa.

It made me never want to be married again. More than not trusting you, it made me not trust myself. I still jump at loud noises; I still have nightmares. The hardest part afterward was realizing that I was the kind of woman who agreed to be hit. "What are you doing with a guy who's going to kill you?" That's what a counsellor once asked me. I couldn't answer the question.

There's an old saying in A.A.: "The rocks in his head fit the holes in hers." That's how I see things between us now. But I'm not that person anymore. You must have suffered too. I forgive you for not being able to be a better person—because I've failed myself, even when I knew and admitted what was wrong. I forgive you for not being the man I dreamed you could be. Forgive me for not leaving you the first time you hit me. I guess we both had some hard lessons to learn. I'm grateful that neither one of us had to die. I release you and forgive myself.

◆

Stan and Frankie were back in the kitchen, and the country tunes were yowling. Outside, the afternoon sky was darkening, the temperature dropping to almost −40. I zipped the scribbler back inside my suitcase and left the room. First the laundry, second the beds, then the showers and garbage. *Now think about something else.*

Cody passed me in the hallway; I watched him go into the Rec Room. He turned his head away from any eye contact, his subtle snub. He was a big boy, pink-cheeked and the youngest Roughneck, maybe 20. I knew his age and job put him at the bottom of the pecking order—the pounding order—and he needed someone like me to look down on. I could easily see him as the classroom nerd, not ugly, not smart, but bland, the round face and round eyes, thick glasses, a gangly snub-nosed kid. He seemed pleasant; I'd watched him at Eric's heels and Trevor's elbow. Still, the put-down belied the blank face. Whenever I saw him, I looked at the floor. Now that Cody had muscles and money, I wasn't going to take any chances around a bad night of teasing from the other boys and a gut full of vodka.

I kicked the wedge under his bedroom door. The pile on the floor was almost as high as Cody's bed. Most of it was laundry—jeans, sweaters, underwear, all in a tangled heap. There were boxes too, five or six, and they caught my eye, the shiny cellophane windows and bright lettering. It was packaging for radio-controlled trucks and Nintendo games. *Toys!* I wanted to cover them up, like Herb's Bible. *Get to work.* As I leaned over the mattress, a groan startled me. The Leasehand's bed was on the other side of the wall—Mark was getting up. And just like that, I remembered the other camps.

TUMBLER RIDGE, 1975

We've been married less than a year. He's been away at his first camp and I fly to Edmonton to meet him for a weekend. He's over an hour late to pick me up, angry, cold, like a stranger. We get a room and get drunk. I'm afraid of him and I want to go home.

When he does come home from camp, my cousins say how much Ron has changed. He's a lot bigger, they say without smiling.

REVELSTOKE, 1978

He works at the dam site and comes home from camp on the weekends. He hates it. I've come up to see what it's like. Stay in my room and wait, he tells me. It's a cell with a blanket and a bunk. Someone is snoring. The walls are so thin I think I can smell his breath. It stinks.

DAWSON CREEK, 1982

"I rolled the truck on the way back to camp. Come up and help me," Ron says. I leave the kids with Mom and fly up. We go out to a restaurant. He's drunk. He argues with the waitress and follows her into the kitchen. She calls the police and they take him away. "Is he always like this?" the police ask. No. Yes. No. I can't answer the question.

SOMEWHERE NORTH, 1983

His buddy tells me about a fight in camp. The other guy grabbed Ron and threw him down the stairs. Ron got his head pounded. I can guess why. In the morning, all the lumps came up. When he comes home, he doesn't talk about life in camp. I don't ask.

When I finished the rooms, it was time to gather the garbage. The boys were all up and the hallway smelled like tobacco lasagna.

"Hey, Barb. How's it going?" Stan popped out of the Rec Room. He had his puffy chef's hat on and a glazed grin of crooked teeth.

"Good. I'm collecting the garbage." His teeth probably drifted because he was missing the eyetooth.

"Like Italian?"

"Sounds great." I smiled and swung the garbage between us.

"Got sausages and garlic bread on the go too. I'd better get back and see how Frankie's doing." He raised his eyebrows and shook his head.

The hallway was no place for standing around. Dan the Driller had to turn sideways to get by us, and he wasn't impressed.

"I'll grab the kitchen garbage now too." I followed Stan through the kitchen door and it was playing again: *I swear I'll change my ways. I just called to say I want you to come back home. I found your picture today . . .*

Frankie was singing and swaying at the counter. She looked up from the buns she was buttering and nodded over the blaring lyrics and fans. I thought her smile looked friendlier. Her garbage was always the heaviest, peelings and cores; Stan's was full of cans, boxes, food wrapping. I heaved two bags out the back kitchen door and geared up to go outside.

"Use my coveralls," called Stan. "And don't stay out too long."

"Don't worry." I leaned around the doorway. "I'll be fast." It was nearly −40 with the wind chill. As I opened the door to the shock of cold, I wondered how far I was from Tumbler Ridge and the ghost of a boy from South Vancouver.

◆

The nightshift boys were back and eating supper. I'd managed a slab of lasagna between the shift changes and now waited in my room for Stan and Frankie to leave the kitchen. A crossword was open in front of me. I'd found a book of puzzles in the Rec Room and had grabbed it for something to fill the time between chores. Generally I hated crosswords. Three down to fit five across—didn't life have enough frustration? I'd get a word that fit another word, and then another, only to realize four words ago was the wrong word. Like writer didn't fit with Frankie and neither did banker. Housecleaner or hostess did. Drunk fit with Ron, but not marriage or children. I had to go back and change words to fit the person. I was stuck.

$800

A thick plank of cheddar waited at Frankie's elbow. She was busy chopping celery. Behind the cheese was a harvest sack of carrots. Around her feet were the usual slops of water on the floor. Frankie was either going to take root or rot where she stood.

"I ain't never gonna be no skinny minny," she called over her shoulder to Stan. They stood back to back, Stan at the stove, Frankie at the sinks. She saw me and raised her voice over the racket. "I'm a big girl." She laughed and shook her hips.

"Morning, Frankie. Morning, Stan." I didn't care if they heard me or not. I'd been ejected from another night of bad dreams.

"Morning, Barb." Stan had on his double-breasted white tunic; he did a snappy grapevine dance step to the Dixie Chicks and saluted me with the flipper. Bacon, sausages and onion were duking it out on the grill for their share of air space. Competition was fierce. The camp was airtight, sealed like syrup.

"Dammit," Frankie said. She held up two blue-gloved hands. "That girl that left here didn't leave any prep for the rig boxes. I had to start from nothing, it put me behind . . . "

"I don't know how you do it." More than a few times I'd wondered how Frankie stood at the counter for hours on end without a break—cocaine? Since the first night she came flying through the kitchen door off the grocery truck, I hadn't seen her step outside the camp building. Oh, there was the night trip to Grande Prairie with Mark. But how did she stay that "up"? The woman didn't seem to get down or even sit down.

I worried. Was her job a lot more work than the campie's job? Or was Stan dumping his work onto her? I stirred the coffee and kept my mouth shut. By now I knew that any words of sympathy or offers of help sounded like a threat to Frankie. And since Stan had offered me her job, I was a threat.

He'd done it again the other morning. "I tell you, at the end of the week, she's outta here," he'd said. "The woman never shuts up—she's driving me fucking crazy."

I knew what he meant. But by then I also knew Stan changed his mind every time he smoked a joint. And I still wasn't sure I wanted her job.

" . . . and the boys are really going to love what I put in the rig box today. I've got some nice chicken drumsticks from last night that they can grab and eat with their hands. Jeez, Stan, you're really burning through the pans this morning, I have to get these rig boxes ready by . . . "

"Come on, Frankie—organize, improvise, prioritize," interrupted Stan.

This was another one of Stan's favourite lines. Coffee in hand, I mumbled an excuse and ducked out to my room to pray in front of an open window. The camp was an oven and I needed to stick my head out of it.

◆

Okay. The door was shut, the window open. I closed my eyes and took a deep breath. And another. Eyes closed, I listened past the kitchen noise until I could hear my heartbeat. *Hear that?* Tha-thump, tha-thump. *That's the most important thing.* Tha-thump. *Keep that going. No matter what.*

Okay. Simple instructions: *stay alive.* I waited for a nudge, a sign, a feeling, a thought, a voice, a good idea, something.

◆

VICTORIA, BC, SEPTEMBER 2001

Dr. K. Lilley, Psychiatrist

He looks like Santa Claus. I've been seeing him for a year now. By this time next year, we'll have inched my Prozac up to 100 milligrams a day. "I get these funny shocks through my body when I go for a run," I tell him. Pshaw. He tells me about colleagues who have patients on doses 10 times what I take. Okay. More Prozac doesn't sound like a bad idea to me. In fact, any idea that pops into my head is a good idea. I don't have any more bad ideas. Mortgaging my house to write a book without a publisher was a great idea. Living off credit cards seemed like another great idea. Now I'm bankrupt. No Prozac problem. Now I'm debt free.

Dr. Lilley asks how I am.

Great, I'm great. I tell him about my recent trip to Nootka Island, how I backpacked a wilderness trail for six days with friends. I don't tell him that I peed myself because I was too exhausted to pull down my pants. Or that I ran out of food on the fourth day so the others had to stretch their rations to share food with me. I tell Dr. Lilley that it rained for four days, but I don't tell him that at the end of every day I ate a T3 for supper and fell into my sleeping bag instead of helping collect firewood and tree the group's food cache from bears. That I found a dirty eagle's feather (it might have been a seagull's), stuck it into my hair and left it there for days. I don't tell him that the trip ruined a long-term friendship because I was jealous and competitive. Nor do I mention that I won't be able to pay my rent next month because I've spent all my money on this great holiday.

My behaviour should terrify me, but Prozac nixes bad ideas like terror. Dr. Lilley wants to talk about my childhood, but I seem to have lost an adult. There was a certain woman who was a bank loans officer, who raised two children on her own, saved her money, cut the lawn, washed her car, paid her debts and lived within her means. I barely remember her. Oh well.

◆

Ah, the relief of the mop: my sweat made a difference. By now I had figured out a system that got the campie's daily chores done in about five hours. That left 19 hours for sleep and . . . well, whatever. As we'd walked through my training, Andy had kept saying, "Take your time." Except slow wasn't my style. I liked Stan's mantra: "organize, improvise, prioritize." I'd found a rhythm to changing beds and washing floors. No one ever walked into a dirty bathroom or reached for a clean towel that wasn't on the shelf. As for the garbage, it was a relief to get outside.

When dayshift finished breakfast, I put away the mop and went into the kitchen.

"Hey, Barb," called Stan, "could I get you to do something for me?"

"Okay . . . what?"

"Would you mind throwing my wash on? There's a laundry bag behind the door in my room."

"Sure, I'll do it this morning." *You weasel.* Andy had warned me not to do anyone else's laundry: "You could get into real trouble for that."

"What'll you have for breakfast, Barb?"

"An omelette would be great, thanks, Stan." I found a place at the long chrome table and watched him at the grill.

Frankie was oddly quiet. She glanced over the sinks and smiled briefly. Her aim with the sprayer wasn't so good; water was ricocheting off the pans and up the wall. I held my breath and waited for her to ask me to do her laundry as well. What would I say? But other than smashing pans in the sinks, she was quiet.

"So I guess Tom's recovered—that was kind of an expensive night," I said.

Frankie's silence unnerved me. Had Stan said something about me taking her job?

"Yeah. Eric said that the lad was looking pretty weak yesterday," said Stan as he handed me a plate. "Toast?"

"Sure, thanks."

"I wish Herb hadn't complained about the rig boxes," said Frankie.

"Fuck 'em," said Stan. "That's what I say. These boys want steak every night. We can't afford that, so fuck 'em."

"Do they make good money out here?" I was relieved to hear Frankie speak up and guessed she was upset about Herb's complaint.

"Riggies make *great* money," said Frankie.

"Yeah, depending on their job. Some of the boys make 500, 600, 700 dollars a day or even more," said Stan. He set a plate beside me.

"Leasehands, drivers, they don't make so much. It depends on their skills. The engineers make big money."

"Wow." I meant the wages, not the toast.

"That's nothing. You know what a guy should do to make some real money up here?" Stan didn't wait for my guess. "Get a motorhome and some girls and go from camp to camp to camp." He laughed and looked out the window, as if he could already see his moneymaking brothel in the parking lot. "Yup. Roll in with the girls, camp to camp. Work all winter and have summers off."

"Whoa," said Frankie, the gloom lifting from her face. "You'd only have to work a coupla months a year." She hooted and did another shimmy. "Let's do it."

"I'll bet somebody's already thought of it," I added. My own eyes had followed Stan's gaze to the parking lot. I imagined a Winnebago, Stan stoned at the wheel, Frankie peeling carrots, and me counting oily hundred-dollar bills into tidy stacks of three. We'd have turquoise postcards tucked into the visors, pink conch shells and a hula dancer on the dash . . . we'd be planning our next tropical suntan.

"I tell you, you'd be rich in no time flat. I don't know of anybody that's doing it. But they should," said Stan. His face was lit up, eyes bright. "It'd be so easy."

"I'm in," said Frankie. "The riggies would love it."

"It'd be *sooo* easy, I've been thinking about . . . " Stan twirled a ladle between two fingers while he fondled the idea.

"You'd be rich in no time for sure," I echoed and took another bite of toast. Outside, the sky was blue and fresh snow had rounded off the camp to a pristine vision of winter beauty. I studied the view from the kitchen but knew the reality: cold killed. Deep in my brain, grey cells registered the difference between fantasy and fact, between a good idea and a bad idea. Already I'd called Stan "John" by mistake. Maybe I was smartening up.

◆

The morning passed as usual. Stan and Frankie disappeared after the nightshift boys passed out. Eager for oxygen, I rounded up the kitchen garbage and pulled on Stan's coveralls. My exit out the door and down the steps was fast, quiet, unseen. The cold bite of clean air felt good on my face, the only exposed skin. This kind of snow was still a novelty, a dry squelch under my boots instead of the coastal slush I'd known all my life. It was a shame to cloud the perfect sky with burning garbage. I dragged the bags and loaded the incinerator. No matter. I had already decided that today I was going to explore the road farther south from camp, in the direction of the rig.

The road, icy and wide, soon fell into a steep downward grade. I strained to listen for engine noise. Every so often I checked over my shoulder, hoping to see only empty road and not the dark shape of a skulking animal in my tracks. *Go away.* I didn't want to ruin the relief of space and solitude by being afraid. What a relief to stretch my legs and walk in a long straight line. Soon I found a rhythm to my stride that matched deep gulps of air. Ahead, I could see the road rise to a crest. No ambiguity, no decisions. Just the sky, the trees and me.

The road dipped across a frozen creek and then the incline sharpened. Still no traffic. I hoped Pete the Tool Push was far away. I started to sweat; I missed being able to go for a run. Yesterday, Stan had made pineapple dessert squares that I couldn't leave alone. The day before that, cheesecake.

My ears ached in the silence. If I still wanted to let loose some choked scream of rage or anguish, this was the place. I spoke aloud. "I need to keep my focus on why I'm here, 'to clear up the wreckage of my past.' I need to write those letters."

I sound phony.

"Do you think anybody except God is listening to me?" I raised my voice. "Who are you fooling with this bullshit?" I almost yelled, "Why can't you ever say what you really think?" The sky didn't even blink. "Who are you arguing with—God or yourself?"

I wasn't sure.

I walked faster. "What if you had a dream but could never reach it because of all the obstacles in the way? And what if one day all the reasons why you couldn't be the person you'd always wanted to be were gone—that finally, nothing stood in the way of what you'd always wanted to do? How do you think it would feel to watch yourself fuck it up? To know that it was no one else's fault. That the thing in the way of your dreams all these years was you."

Tears and snot froze on my face. "Well, look around, Barbara." I did. "That's why you're here. That's why you feel the way you feel. You stood in your house and asked yourself, 'Whose dream is this?' And then you tore down your life."

I hoped God would overhear, interrupt, disagree, take the blame.

Are houses and possessions the only ballast that keeps us from drifting away? What about refugees, prisoners, victims of war or disaster, people stripped of everything?

I imagined the weight of nothing. What if my name was my only possession? Camp life was hard. Yet for me, bed and board were a simple about-face on the road. Canada was no third-world country. I was a soft white-skinned woman protected by medical coverage and law.

Being out here alone in the wilderness was a risk, but if someone raped me, a superior officer wouldn't applaud or reward the conquest. If I was murdered and my body stashed in the trees, the law would eventually register my loss. Bankruptcy was tough. But I had not lost my children, my sobriety, my citizenship, my health. This place was dangerous for women and men; I could see that. But my life still had weight.

A certain woman in Africa would never know how Stan had carried her story to me. She would never know how many times a day I wondered if she was one woman or hundreds of women, alone and naked because she'd sold her body for seven dollars and 30 days. She would never know, if she existed at all, that her suffering was the down payment to understanding my right-sized problem.

It was time for an about-face. I kept to the left, facing traffic, walking in the curdled snow for better footing. I wondered about the boxes left in my uncle's Quesnel basement. Every move whittled more away. I considered the revolutionary idea that loss might not be a bad thing.

The weight of the house and its contents settled on a point between my shoulder blades. In the year before bankruptcy, I gave away, threw away or sold almost everything, because it looked like more than I could carry. I thought it would crush me. The year after the bankruptcy, I had to move my boxes six times. My possessions are scattered. Now there are remnants of furniture in my mother's basement, boxes of Christmas decorations in my sister's Langley barn. My best linen disappeared off the back of a pickup truck in Victoria. I have Rubbermaid totes of clothes and dishes in Quesnel. The laptop and printer froze in the logger's old travel trailer. Aunty Madge has my camera equipment in her bedroom closet. I sent my daughter Melissa my best jewellery, just in case. No wonder I feel all apart.

Where the hill crested, the view was aerial, the landscape undulating to the distant Rocky Mountains. I clambered off the road and into the trees toward a knoll. I was hoping for a clearing, a private place away from the threat of traffic. In a matter of yards, the trees opened to a bare rock cliff. I stood with the sun on my face and looked to the west and home.

I stared at the Rockies until they became transparent. On the other side, I saw a woman named Barbara who lived in Victoria. I watched her shopping here and there, the trips to Mexico, Ottawa, Calgary, visiting friends across the country. I saw her give away and throw away money and time that she needed for herself. From here, she looked like a fool, unemployed, living off credit and pipe dreams. For the first time, I saw myself outside of myself. This was the objective view—judgment based simply on behaviour, not motives or intentions. Who could have read my mind? My decisions didn't make sense; my actions looked irresponsible. It looked like I deserved what I got.

The mountains pulled at my heart and called me home. I wanted to memorize the sight of them. I was afraid to move and lose the insight I'd gained. But fear started to poke at my back. It was time to leave. I walked the road back to camp thinking about street people and the limits of love and cash and telepathy.

◆

Smoky kitchen voices mingled with "Since you've been gone" while I unlaced my boots. The door to my room was open.

"Yeah, well Pete says we've got maybe another couple of weeks . . . " Stan was leaning on my bed, talking on the radio phone. I tossed my gloves on the shelf and gave him a wave. He nodded. I didn't know where to go; I didn't like him on my bed. Reluctantly, I wandered into the kitchen.

Dan the Driller and Cody the young Roughneck were at the table. Mark was leaning on the counter beside Frankie.

"Hey, Barb, you're back," said Frankie. "Where did you go?"

"Oh, just down the road a little ways. It's so beautiful out . . . " I stopped. Frankie was making a strange face, kind of a half grin with a raised eyebrow. I got the feeling my walk had already been a topic of discussion.

"I couldn't go out there—it's dangerous, you know. And besides, I need to get some sleep on our breaks. Stan and I start work so early in the morning, you know, before anyone else gets up. And I look forward to having fun with the guys at night. When I'm at home I go to the gym and work out every day. I've got a special routine. See—I've got great upper-body strength." Frankie flexed her arm to prove it.

"Oh yeah," said Mark. "You're a strong girl." He laughed and lit a cigarette.

Dan and Cody laughed as well, while Frankie posed at the counter.

"Say, did you hear one of the guys from Beaver say that they saw a grizzly the other day?" asked Dan.

"Really?" said Cody.

"Yeah—the guy said it had a head on him the size of an oil barrel."

"No shit."

Was it a joke on me? I pretended that I didn't hear and left the kitchen to find some laundry. The door closed on the laughter behind me.

"Hi, Stan." I met him coming out of my room. "I heard what you were saying when I came in—is the camp going to move?"

"It's in the works. Pete'll let us know."

"What happens to us? Have you moved with a camp before?"

"Oh God, yes. It's a huge job—you work your ass off. Everything has to be packed." He rolled his eyes.

"Everything?"

"The whole camp."

"We do it?"

"It's part of your job—take down and set up. It's a huge job. All the dishes, the whole kitchen has to be boxed up, everything. When that's done, they take the trailers apart and tow them to the next site. And then you start all over. Unpack everything, the whole camp. Fuck, it's a lot of work. I try to miss it but if it happens when you're here, you gotta do it."

I made a face. It sounded like hell. "Do you think I'll be here when the camp moves?"

"Well, do you want Frankie's job?"

"Is the pay better than the campie's job?"

"What are they paying you now?"

"A hundred dollars a day."

"Fuck!" Stan pulled a face. "Is that all? I wouldn't even get out of bed for that."

I waited for Stan to tell me what he would get out of bed for . . .

"Yeah, the cook's helper makes more than that. Fuck, anybody makes more than that."

"How much more?" I was starting to feel stupid.

"I don't know. But more than that. Phone Legacy and ask." Stan ran his hands through his hair. "I gotta get going on supper. Let me know what you're gonna do. Jason needs to know if Andy's coming back here or not." He shrugged and turned for the kitchen door.

The Rec Room door opened and Old Tom came out, mug in hand. He looked at me without speaking and then lurched to the right. I hoped he wasn't going back to his room. All of nightshift should be up by now and I needed to change the beds. Nope. It looked like he was falling toward the bathroom. I armed myself with Windex and a big garbage can for the next round of smashing mattresses.

◆

The boys were having hamburgers for supper. I sat at the desk in my room with my eyes closed and scanned the horizon for the Rockies. It was time for the next letter.

Dear Janice,

I forgive you for working hard, succeeding at your job, being financially successful, for moving on and making new friends at your own level of confidence and wealth. I forgive you for a better childhood than my own, for your ambition, your home, your car, your clothes. I forgive your knowledge and education. I forgive your physical strengths and your thick blond hair.

I forgive you for succeeding where I have failed. I forgive you for resisting temptations that overcame me—no—that I gave in to and got fat and broke. I forgive your self-discipline. I resented the contrast of your life to mine. I forgive you for exposing my motives, my jealousy. I forgive you for all the holidays you've taken, and especially I forgive you for all that I imagine you have now, the great times you have with wonderful friends I'll never meet.

I forgive you for your future. Most of all, I forgive you for leaving me behind.

It was wrong to compare myself to you. I judged you on nothing more than what I could see from the outside. I looked at your behaviour from a distance and drew my own sour conclusions without knowing all the facts. I assumed that because I knew parts of you and some of your history—that I knew all of you. I was wrong.

I now choose to release you from all of my resentment and self-pity. I forgive myself for not accepting and loving the woman God made me to be.

I put down the pen. Even as I wrote, I knew this letter could have been addressed to almost every woman friend I'd ever had, right back to grade school. One by one I saw their faces and heard my complaint, "I'd be happy if I had her . . . whatever." It occurred to me now that it would be a shame if I never met another man or woman as an equal. What a shame if I heard nothing but "you're not good enough." I wondered what that listening part was called, and while I was scratching my head, looking at the wall, suddenly, on the other side of my closed door, Stan said loudly, "Has anyone seen Barb?"

"I'm right here, Stan—did you need me for something?" I opened the door and faced him.

"Fuck no—I thought you'd gone outside again for a walk." He half laughed in that twisted way that could have been an insult or a compliment. "It's 40 below out there—the lads say it's really blowing tonight.

Don't want you out there lost." His light blue eyes were shiny pink. He was stoned goofy.

"No. Don't worry, Stan. I'll wash the floor now, if you and Frankie are done . . . " I leaned to look over his shoulder and into the kitchen.

"You betcha." He spun on his heel and yanked open the Rec Room door. It took him in a single bite.

$900

Stan's gone berserk. He jumped, he hopped, he jerked like a toy man on a string. Steel fry pans crashed onto the grill. I stood back. Bacon and eggs flew out of his hands, out of his sleeves, while he double-timed it between the stove, the fridge, the cupboards and back again. The man had knives or else I would have laughed. He spotted me.

"Fuckin' Frankie's slept in—will you go bang on her door?" He shook his hands at the stove. "She's put me way behind."

His hair was in clumps, his eyes bulging and bloodshot. I looked at the clock—5:30 a.m.—he was an hour behind schedule. *Frankie's fault?* The boys would be ready for breakfast at six and the grill was stone cold. Even I knew the massive stove took time to get hot. It would be ugly. Complaints about the food were constant. *No food* would be grounds for a pounding. The hungover boys might beat Stan up. If even scrawny Blake hit him once, I'd have to look for Stan in the snowbank across the parking lot.

"Sure thing, Stan." Off to the rescue: through the pantry, around the corner, past the laundry to the door labelled *Cook's Helper*, beside the camp generator. I stopped. Knocking on bedroom doors had always made me extremely anxious—like poking a stick into a cave to see if there was a sleeping grizzly inside. I took a deep breath and knocked. Nothing. No surprise. Who'd hear anything over that generator? I knocked harder.

"Frankie—it's Barb. Are you awake? Hello? Good morning, Frankie." *Rap, rap, rap.* "Frankie? Are you in there?" My voice warbled, irrationally choked. This was no time for long explanations or therapy. "Frankie!"

The door recoiled. I felt the suction. Frankie gripped the frame; it held her up. She was tousled.

"What time's it?" The top of Frankie's head did the talking and not very clearly. She faced the floor.

"It's after 5:30. Stan sent me to get you. Are you okay?" I peered over her shoulder into the dark room for another body. Other than strangled sheets, the bed was empty.

"Shit. Oh shit." She rubbed her forehead with the back of her hand. "Tell him I'll be right there." Without looking up, she closed the door.

Okay. Back to the kitchen I went. Stan was a pale frenetic blur, cigarette in one hand, flipper in the other, pushing bacon, scrambling eggs, buttering toast. The hot trays were steaming.

"She's coming," I said lightly. "Can I help with anything?"

"Yeah. Can you start cutting up cheese and celery for the rig boxes?" He raised his eyebrows and pulled a face. "Did you wake her up?"

"Yup. Is the cheese in this fridge or that one?" I didn't want to say anything more about Frankie because I knew she'd come barrelling through the door at any minute.

"I'm calling Jason today—this is bullshit," Stan said. "I've had it with her." But some of the fire had gone out of his voice. It looked as though he'd made the save and had something to put on the plates when the boys came in for breakfast. "The cheese is in that fridge over there," he said and pointed to the one across from the tables and closest to me. "Tell me today if you want her job. And don't worry—I can teach you everything you need to know. The job's not that hard."

"Okay." I glanced at the clock.

"Maybe get the coffee going too," Stan added.

I had more questions but now wasn't the time to ask them. Besides, could I trust Stan to help me make a decision? He'd probably say anything to get me to take the job. But every time he smoked up, he changed his mind about Frankie. What if I gave up my campie job and he changed his mind about me? Andy would come back and I'd be the odd one out. Would Legacy send me home or would they give me work at another camp? I poured water into the coffee maker and measured the Maxwell House. Where was home? *Auuggh.* I needed time to think. Never mind flaky Stan. How could I trust my own judgment?

Another clock check. Provided Frankie showed up soon, there'd still be enough time to give the Rec Room a fast wipe before the boys were up. I rummaged through the fridge, tucked the cheddar under one arm, bundles of celery under the other. Both sinks were full of tangled whisks and mixing bowls; I needed them free for washing vegetables. How did Frankie work in this mess? I emptied one sink into the other and moved the cutting board and knife block closer. My fingers gripped the blade handle. I loved this kind of working prayer, the practical offering of celery.

Fat fried to the steady rotation of the hood fans. Stan tapped the radio switch as Frankie came swinging through the door.

"Sorry, Stan. My alarm didn't go off—that clock radio in my room isn't working right—I'm gonna get a new one when I'm on my break next week." Frankie paused and frowned when she saw me. "Thanks, Barb. You can go now. I'll get this."

"Are you sure? I can finish cutting up this celery for the rig boxes while you start something else," I offered.

"No thanks," Frankie said, her voice firm. "You've got your own work to do." She stood at the counter, arms folded, and waited for me to leave. She wasn't going to do anything until I got out of her way.

"Okay." I put down the knife, wiped my hands and smiled at Frankie's drawn face. She forced a smile back. Stan nodded as I left the kitchen.

●

Herb was smouldering in the Rec Room.

"Good morning," I said.

"Uhuh." He was staring at the television. It wasn't on.

"I'm a little late today." I smiled, sort of, and scooped an armload of beer cans. When I dumped the cigarette butts, ash flew up into the air and settled in the back of my throat. The taste reminded me of when I was a newcomer at AA meetings. The old-timers told me to empty the ashtrays after the meeting ended. They knew the small task paid big dividends in sobriety. Among other things, it kept me from running out the door. It also gave Marguerite time to corner me.

I was 30 years old and two days sober when Marguerite walked over and introduced herself. We were in the Courtenay Alano Club. My hands were shaking. She said, "The train's going to the dump—why don't you get off now?"

VICTORIA, OCTOBER 2000

It's a beautiful day for the three-hour drive from Victoria north to Courtenay. She is in a small brown box on the seat beside me in the truck. "We're taking our last drive together, Marguerite,"

I say. She died 32 years sober. How she'd love the irony of the plain brown wrapper, her last outfit. I am taking her home to her husband, Mel, and her daughters, Grace and Linda. They are going to scatter her ashes on Long Beach, in a cove north of Ucluelet. I know the very spot.

WICKANINNISH, AUGUST 1988

The AA rally is at the hall in Ucluelet. We drive from Courtenay and stay at Tin Wis, an old First Nations residential school, now run by the band. It's right on the beach; our room has bunk beds. Tonight, the rally membership will put on a seafood feast and we'll dance till midnight.

After morning coffee at the Wickaninnish Inn, we walk the beach: Marguerite, her daughter Grace with her school chum Christine, my sponsee, Arlene. We pick shells and skip waves like girls. Marguerite stops at a cove. We wait while she lingers. Beauty is everywhere—the expanse of blue sky, the surf, intricate sand patterns—but something about this cove holds Marguerite.

"Come on," she calls us over. "Let's say the Third Step prayer here." The five of us hold hands, kneel and repeat together, "God, I offer myself to thee, to build with me and do with me as thou wilt. Relieve me of the bondage of self, that I may better do thy will. Take away my difficulties, that victory over them may bear witness to those I would help of thy power, thy love, and thy way of life. May I do thy will always."

My knees in the sand, the salt air on my tongue, Marguerite's baritone and the firm grip of her hand: the prayer anchors deep.

We get up, brush off our knees, laugh, stroll on, our wills sur-
rendered to a fancy for ice cream.

VICTORIA, OCTOBER 2000

Nothing prepares me for the drive back to Victoria without the
little brown box. How can I explain my grief? I can't say that
she was my mother, my sister, a lover or even my best friend.
Marguerite was my sponsor for 15 years. She was a part of my
daily life, AA meetings, visiting at her house or mine, talking
on the phone for hours about how to clean up my life and take
care of my kids. I always said, "She pushed up her shirt sleeves
and got into the mess of my life. She helped me find the way out
of hell." How can I describe my loss?

I drive home and expect a season of sadness and tears
(the cliché of grief) while I carry on with life. After a couple
of months, a stranger appears in my home. She hijacks my
life. She seeks lower companions. She smashes things that
are important to me. She throws away money and saves the
worthless. I try to keep her happy and give her everything she
wants. She almost destroys me. I think she wants to kill me.
She is inconsolable.

•

Maybe Herb saw something in that blank television screen, or maybe
it was just his place to sit unmolested and dream about the wife back
home and the five-year plan. Perhaps there was a congregation praying
in tongues for Herb and rebuking the camp demons. I doubted much,
spirit or otherwise, would pierce his shield of smoke. Still, why chance

the crossfire? I decided to vacuum the Rec Room later. Out in the hallway, I listened: all three showers were in use. That meant a couple of the boys were either still in bed or already in the kitchen. *Improvise.* I wanted to brush my teeth and shower off the ash. I wanted to look at Marguerite's picture and start the day over. Somewhere else as someone else. I dithered.

No dice. Young Tom passed me in the hallway, bleary-eyed and wet. Roughneck Dave wasn't far behind. Neither spoke; I wasn't sure they'd even seen me against the wall. But I saw two empty bathrooms ready to clean.

Over the past couple of days, I'd noticed that Dave seemed to spend more time in the kitchen around Frankie than anyone else. It was irritating to steer the garbage and laundry around him, the big lug, and listen to his goofy banter. Was he the reason Frankie's clock didn't work this morning? It might be fun to join the boys in the evening—to see what went on in the Rec Room with Frankie and Stan.

But so far the camp nightlife was beyond my earplugs and barricaded door. That big rubber band of tension was wound up tight, and my brain would never let me forget how to make it relax. How many nights could I watch everybody else smoke and drink? Years of seeing other alcoholics relapse had taught me that sobriety was a gift with an unknown expiry date. How long would I get away with it? One night? Two weeks? Four months? It didn't matter. I knew the outcome never changed—a drunk got drunk. Of course, there was the question of my welcome in the Rec Room: few who enjoyed drinking the way these boys did wanted to be around some dud who didn't drink.

Andy's squeegee did a good job on the shower walls. I wiped them down and then worked on my knees backward out of the bathroom.

When I turned to reach for my bucket in the hallway, Trevor the Driver was standing behind me.

"Oh, sorry—are you waiting for this bathroom?"

"Yep."

"I'm all done. Just watch the floor—it's *really* wet." I hoped he'd say something like, "Okay, I'll use the other bathroom," because why make me have to clean this one again before the shift change?

"No prob." He stepped over my bucket and onto the wet floor.

◆

From the sanctuary of my room, things sounded back to normal in the kitchen, the usual ruckus of morning shift change. I could hear Frankie laughing and Stan yelling, "Hey, Cody, have the works in that omelette?" I'd already been out under the seductive black blanket of a trillion stars and burned the garbage. I gawked. Took it all in. Couldn't get enough. Head-to-toe shivers. It was a long cold bottomless drink in a barren wilderness. A gulp before I trudged back into the smoky little box.

The washer and dryer were going; I retreated to my room between loads. The radio phone watched me. Stan said he was going to call Jason at Legacy today. It was decision time. No matter what Stan did or didn't do about Frankie, I still needed to figure things out for myself. Was there a life here for me? Was there a better way to make more money? Should I get an apartment in Grande Prairie? With no money, no furniture—with what? I pulled out the scribbler hidden in my suitcase. If I didn't decide on a course of action, I knew that boredom and loneliness would eventually drive me into the oblivion of the Rec Room. Once, during a meditation, I'd heard these words: *You'll never be so saintly that you weren't a drunk.* It was a reminder that while the spirit was willing, the flesh was even more willing.

Nobody was likely to need me for anything, but still, I left my door partially open. Pen in hand, I started to write.

When you have no choice but to stay put, you can either use the time and confinement to your advantage or let the time destroy you. What are the advantages of being in camp?
- *freedom from distraction*
- *enforced savings*
- *freedom from social obligations*
- *a time out*

I thought about life in Victoria, how I'd wished for more time to exercise and the will to avoid coffee shop goodies. Camp isolation offered one and removed the other. What did I weigh now? How could I keep track without a scale or measuring tape? I surveyed the room. On the floor were sacks of clean sheets, closed—aha!—with string. I tied three string lengths together to make one, pulled it around my waist and marked my size on the string with a black felt pen. I stretched out the string and guessed my circumference was a few inches shy of three feet. Stan's dessert squares were rounding me off.

I turned back to the scribbler.

I need to keep my focus on why I'm here, on what the prize is, the money to pay off my debts . . .
- *Student Loans—$10,000*
- *Dr. Lilley—$100*

- Darlene—$65 for long-distance phone calls
- Uncle Rob—$10

I can choose the hard way and feel good or choose the easier softer way and feel disgusted with myself. The time will pass.

Meanwhile, where was home? I couldn't go back to the trailer in Quesnel and I couldn't face my family in Langley. Then it occurred to me. I was asking the wrong question—not where to live but where to work.

I don't want Frankie's job and I sure don't want her room. I don't want Andy's cursing and smoking.

I needed God with a calculator, my debt divided by $100 days. Six months in camp, less tax and living expenses, would get me on my feet again. I stretched out on the floor and did 10 sit-ups. It was getting light outside. Nightshift must be finished with the showers. *Make a decision.* My belly rolled over the top of my sweatpants. *Look at the size of your waist and the size of your waste.* I decided to take Frankie's job.

There was a tap at my door.

"Yes?" I scrambled up off the floor.

Frankie leaned into the room. "Are you okay? Stan wants to know if there's something wrong." Her brow was creased—she glanced around the room.

I was startled to see her out of the kitchen and stood up in front of the desk to hide the scribbler. "Oh no, just reading. I'm fine." I tried to sound casual. "In a few minutes I'm going to clean the bathrooms." And for good measure added, "It's hard to be away. I miss my kids."

Frankie clucked and made a sympathetic face. The window put

light into her dark almond eyes. "Yeah, I miss my roommate. Lucky guy, he's got the whole condo to himself while I'm away in camp." She pushed her hair back behind one ear. "Dammit, he must love that. He can play his tunes loud and do whatever he wants, have all his buddies over." Something caught her attention; she looked back over her shoulder, behind the door. "Hi, Dave—how many days have you been in camp now?"

From behind the door I heard something like "17 days." I didn't care. This was the first time anyone had come looking for me. Maybe I wasn't as invisible as I had believed. The thought made me feel a little better and a little worse. It was nice to feel cared about—but why did they care?

Frankie had turned away to compare tours of duty with Dave. My room started to shrink; I needed to get out. "Excuse me, Frankie." She stepped aside and I slithered down the hallway to scrub the toilets.

My hands knew their way around a bowl rim; I was intimate with the treachery of loose bolts and curves that hugged scum. Shiny chrome taps were especially satisfying. The work made me feel powerful; I played house with little-girl metaphors. Fantasy was so much a part of my thought-life that I wondered, dimly, if I had confused fantasy with faith. Did I substitute wishful thinking for real work and call it "waiting for God"? Is that why I had gone bankrupt?

Three times a day I cleaned those fixtures on my hands and knees, a pattern of genuflection. Men always splattered pee at a certain height on the wall beside the toilet. It dried as a thick yellow paste and was hard to scrub off. That's exactly where I was, on my knees, contemplating God and meditating on the three-word psalm of my survival: work, work, work.

·

Sometimes other men working in the area stopped in for lunch. Today was one of those days. Strange men were eating at the kitchen tables.

"It's a courtesy," explained Stan. "I mean, where else are they going to get something to eat out here?" He waved at the window, the wall of trees and snow outside. "Our guys can do the same thing—they could walk into the kitchen at Beaver camp and get supper, no problem." He paused to flip a dozen or so grilled cheese sandwiches, then lifted the basket of golden fries from the bubbling deep fryer. "All the camps do it for each other."

"No charge? You mean free meals?"

Stan saw a dolt. "Well, ya-ah."

"Wow." No wonder the boys heaved full plates, food and all, into the garbage.

I looked at the men across the table and recognized one of the engineers who had been here before with Pete the Tool Push. He had a friendly face so I decided to say hello.

"Hi, how are you doing? Stan makes a pretty mean cherry pie, doesn't he?"

The engineer swallowed a mouthful and smiled at me. "It's great—hard on the waistline though." He rubbed his plaid flannel belly and laughed. It was an easy laugh.

Encouraged, I introduced myself and asked him for his name again.

"It's Ray. I remember you—you're the new campie. How are you finding it out here?"

"Oh, it's a big change from Victoria . . . but I really needed the work."

He laughed. We talked about the weather, the economy and camp life. I mentioned the campie job was a great start but I'd like to find work that, well, you know, paid a little better. But I didn't know how to find out or who'd know about other kinds of work that a woman could do out here . . .

He nodded, listened, took a sip of coffee and then said, "Well, we might need someone to take night readings for us . . ."

"What kind of readings?"

"From the rig. You'd have to work nights though. But you could do that."

"What exactly is the job?"

"Easy. You check the gauges and record the readings. It has to be done four times a night, but that's all you do. Climb up, check the gauges and record what they say. The company will give you a truck."

"Do you know how much it pays?"

"About $300 a shift. It's steady nights though."

"Just to take down recordings? How do I find out about it?"

"I can ask when I'm back at the office. I can find out where they need somebody and recommend you."

"That'd be fantastic. When do you think you'd know?" I was thinking about Frankie leaving, Andy coming back, and me getting out of here to triple my wages. And a truck! Was this God's answer to my prayers?

"I'll be back early next week, so in a couple of days."

"Wow, thanks, Ray. I know I could do the job. I used to work in a bank and I'm really good—you know, careful—with numbers." I smiled. No. Beamed.

"Sure thing." Ray pushed back his plate, drained his cup and checked his watch. "Well, I'd better be off and see where Pete's at . . . "

I said goodbye and floated to my room to cut up fresh cardboard boxes to tape onto the floor. The mat took about an hour to piece together at the camp doorway. Meanwhile, the scenario of my salvation unfolded: my company truck was brand new, like Dan the Driller's club cab. A clipboard rested on the steering column. The radio was on and so was the heater and I was dividing my debt into $300 nights and easy days.

•

Stan and Frankie finally left the kitchen for the night. I stacked the chairs, washed the floor and turned out the lights. Thick smoke oozed from the Rec Room. The party was on. Tonight I was writing another letter.

Dear Marguerite,

I miss you more than a limb. Do you remember the picture I took of you on the back porch in Victoria? I have that picture with me now. Every day I look into your eyes and I feel found.

I know that you did not want to die. You fought for every breath. You wanted to fight the cancer. You'd been a fighter all your life. But the doctor was trying to tell you and Mel that the fight was over, that it was too late, the cancer had spread. I took my turn beside your bed, talked to you, prayed for you, and after three days, just when I left your room, you died.

I never would have left Ron if you hadn't taken the kids and me into your home. You told me over and over that I didn't deserve to be hit. You pushed me to stand up for myself. "Get mad," you said. While I was raising Melissa and Brian, you were raising me. You taught me that love is what love does.

I never would have stayed sober without you. There's a picture on my fridge: your sponsor Grace, you, my sponsee, and me: our four generations of recovery. Remember the story you told me about the day your sponsor Grace met you at the train station? You had just left the treatment centre and had all your worldly possessions in one box. You said the lid came off a saltshaker and left a long trail of salt behind you. Salt means something more than salt. I knew it even then.

I never told you that one day I drove by that house on Anderton that you and Mel had rented. By then, you had already moved out to Black Creek. Anyway, I saw that the new people had fixed up the front yard and weeded the flowerbed. The first thing I thought was, "Boy, it sure never looked like that when Marguerite lived there." The next thought was this: "That's because you were Marguerite's garden."

I promise to stay sober and keep going to meetings. Thank you for Melissa and Brian. You changed their lives because you saved mine. I forgive you for not being able to stop smoking. I forgive you for leaving me. I love you.

◆

The pain closed like hands around my throat. I cried without making a sound. Grief was not going to leave me; it was going to grow into my soul. There would never be "now I feel better," as if Marguerite had not died. Now I knew grief was closer to insanity and took jackboots to common sense. Where had there been a place for my outrage, my anger at the unfairness of her death? I remembered sobbing on the phone to a long-distance friend when I'd realized the seriousness of Marguerite's cancer and saying, "I feel like half of the planet has blown away." But it was the half hidden from public view, from even family and friends. I realized that John, living in my apartment, measuring hours and heroin, sleeping on the floor beside my bed, was the concrete evidence of my anonymous sorrow.

Death had taken more than Marguerite. Now I knew that it had taken parts of me too. *Who am I now?* I didn't know. But I was going to bed one more day sober.

$1,000

"Blake is pissed because you threw out his pot."

"What?" I didn't like Stan's tone of voice.

"It was in his ashtray and you threw it out."

He made it sound like I'd gone righteous, maybe poured out his booze and burned the girlie magazines too.

"I'll tell Blake that I'm sorry—I guess I didn't see it." There probably *was* a big fatty in his ashtray. Maybe I *did* see it. So what? I wanted to say, "No, I smoked it and it was great!" Instead I heaved the kitchen garbage bags off the back porch into the snow. Then I turned and made a sorry face. "Is anyone else mad at me?"

Stan brightened. "Oh, hell no. The boys really like having you here—you're way better than Andy was. He drove them fuckin' crazy. He was always riding their asses about shit and stuff in their rooms."

Stan scoured the grill as he spoke, his body arched to follow his arms across the wide plates of black steel. He rocked on his toes to the *shhh-shhh* score of the bristles, his pelvis gyrating to the tight metallic circles. The proportions of man to stove reminded me of a jockey around a hot horse. I could see the rote of his touch, how he adjusted dials and dismantled racks to put the stove to bed. I cleaned a toilet the same way, my hands always a wipe ahead of me.

"Honestly, I don't know what the hell Andy did when he was here. He sat in that Rec Room all day, hogging the TV. The boys couldn't watch anything else when he was in there."

"What? You mean they couldn't change the channel if they wanted to watch something else?"

"No way."

"Wow. I can't imagine doing anything like that . . . " But I could imagine Andy with one thumb on the Windex trigger, the other on the fucking remote.

Stan rolled his towel and fired it across the kitchen into the laundry bin. He gave the sinks a pointed look. A greasy mountain of dirty bowls and baking sheets peaked just below the cupboards. Frankie had gone to take a shower, one of her rare breaks from the counter, at the same time every day, right after breakfast. Then, blink, with her hair still wet, she'd be back at it, chopping vegetables.

I worried. Was the job too much work or was Frankie too slow? Too stoned? Or was it something dumb like she didn't own a hair dryer? I toyed with the idea that Stan had loaded her up with work because she hadn't put out—at least not to him. As I slipped the new garbage bag into place, I snuck a look at Stan's skinny ass; he was restacking spices on the ledge beside the stove. The thought of his hopeful little penis jabbing into my belly, his breath heaving through those rotten teeth into my ear . . . did that pothead think I was next? Is that how a cook's helper *really* helped the cook? *And* kept her job? Surely Stan knew that I wasn't game. Even John had boasted that he'd never had to "suck cock for heroin," although he'd chastised me for not taking advantage of my sexuality. "That's a card you've never played well," he'd observed.

I looked at the kitchen space carefully and tried to imagine hours in here alone with Stan. Only now, when I considered the sink full of dirty pans in terms of myself, did I realize something was missing.

"Why doesn't the camp kitchen have a dishwasher?"

"They use up too much water." Stan peeled off his tunic. "That's why we have cook's helpers—*they* do the dishes." He looked at the sinks, rolled his eyes and pulled out a smoke.

It seemed like the right time to take the plunge. "I've decided that I'd like to do the cook's helper job. But I'm worried about Frankie. What'll happen to her?"

"You have? Good. I'll let Jason know you're staying. Don't worry about her." He jerked his head in the direction of the sinks. "Legacy'll send her to a different camp after her break. No problem."

"Well, I feel kinda crappy about it, but I really need to make more money, I'm flat broke . . . "

Stan flushed. "Look, she's got shit all over the place"—he pointed his cigarette at slops on the floor—"and she can't keep up. I need those pans clean at lunch or I'm gonna be washing them myself. And I'm *the cook—I* don't do dishes."

"Okay. Well, if I start when Frankie leaves, when will it be my break?"

"You've done a week already?

"Yup."

"Two more weeks. You can stay longer if you want, but usually it's three in and one out."

"And what about Andy? Will he come back here when I take Frankie's job?"

Stan closed his fingers around the cigarette and took a drag. He blew the smoke out sideways. "Maybe. But probably not. I'll tell Jason the boys don't like him."

"So it really matters that the guys here like the staff?"

"Well, shit, sure. I mean, think about it." Stan made his dummy face at me. "What do you want to see when you come through that door after 12 hours of busting your ass? They're tired and they don't want to put up with any crap. It makes a *big* difference how the boys feel about the camp, that everybody's getting along and it's a good mood in here."

"Oh sure, I can see that. Well, I'm a hard worker, Stan. I know how to organize my time. I'm sure that I could do a good job for you."

"You know it." He shot a look up at the clock. "I don't know where she is but I'm gonna get some shut-eye." The tunic hit the basket— *thwack.* "We'll talk some more later." He left the kitchen with a brisk step, whistling.

Whistling! I had a theory about why men whistled. Either they had just been laid or they believed they were about to be laid. It was a distressing sound coming from Stan.

I looked over the job site. The pans that needed to be scoured; the tangle of ladles, flippers, knives; the bowls of forks and spoons in scummy grey water; crooked stacks of dinner plates yellowed with egg yolk. Frankie had a shitload of work to do before she'd get off her feet. Before lunch. One of the last things Stan had done before he left the kitchen was drop a 50-pound sack of potatoes on the floor in front of the sink. I considered doing the dishes right now. No. Maybe later I'd ask if Frankie wanted some help. Meanwhile, I'd burn the morning garbage—full of the carrots and celery she'd peeled and chopped for the rig boxes the day before. The boys didn't want to eat their vegetables. What a waste. Who made up this menu anyway?

•

Trevor was on the grader in the parking lot. The machine was a yellow and black behemoth, moving fast, pushing snow. I stayed at the edge and waited until I was sure Trevor had seen me wave before I towed the garbage bags across his path to the incinerator. He was a small figure in a high cage, a glint in the eyeball. The grader's horsepower reverberated through my bones. I'd just closed the door on the morning Rec Room party, a-thumping to the usual howls. My brains sizzled like bacon on Stan's grill. I slammed the incinerator door, turned the dial, listened for the *whomp* and decided to find a quiet place before going back inside, maybe on one of the less-travelled side roads. It had warmed up to an almost balmy −20.

I made a left turn at the driveway and walked about half a kilometre. Where the road and its traffic turned left, a spur opened to the right. Only one set of tire tracks had marked the snow. Perfect. I followed them for a few hundred metres to where the truck had stopped, backed up and driven out on the same tracks. At the turnaround point, the driver had gotten out of the truck. I followed boot prints to the piss in the snow. Of course.

Crystalline evergreens bordered the road. The light was perfect. Ravens called. I began to compose a photograph. My camera equipment was in Quesnel, left behind for safekeeping in Aunty Madge's trailer. It would have been worth the risk of losing everything to have had the camera here with me now. Within the scene, a tranquil logic existed in contrast to my interior bedlam. There was nothing ambiguous about daylight and season. The shadowed outcomes were predictable, the forecast of spring inevitable. There was nothing like the real world to calm a fevered brain.

◆

Trevor and his machine had the site cleaned up. I stayed close to the building and kicked the bottom step to knock off the snow before going back inside. One last deep breath, one last look at the trees and sky, heavy with snow and cloud: a place like this could kill or cure a person.

◆

"Dammit!" Frankie let loose a deep belly laugh.

I was in the hallway outside the kitchen door, fumbling with the zipper on Stan's coveralls while trying not to step in puddles of melted snow on the cardboard mats.

"Yeah. Well, I'll let you know, Stan."

I recognized Pete's voice about the same time his collie came around the corner. The dog accepted my pat and went back into the kitchen. For a moment I debated what to face next—laundry or Pete? I remembered Stan's words about the boys wanting "a good mood in here."

"Hi, everybody." Mark and Cody were at the table with Pete. They nodded over coffee mugs in my direction. Pete ignored me.

"Hi, Barb," called Frankie. "I almost made it out before the camp move, dammit! I've been *so-oo* lucky. I've never had to do it before. In all the other camps I worked, they moved on my break when I was away, so I missed out on all the hard work. Dammit!" She had her forearms on the counter for support while she laughed her head off.

"What? We're moving?" I looked at Stan.

"No. Frankie, we don't know that yet for sure," said Stan. He stood in front of the spitting grill, turning wieners and buns with long chrome tongs. "Pete's gonna let us know tomorrow—right?" He looked over at Pete.

"Yeah." He had a knuckle around a coffee mug, one leg hooked under the chair and the other stretched out to trip someone. The collie was under the table, eyes glued to Pete's free hand.

Mark leaned over and said something to Pete. He grunted a reply. Cody had assumed the same slack-jawed posture as Pete.

"They're moving the rig tomorrow—so it depends on where that's at," Stan said.

"Well, I've only got two days left before my break and then I'm off. I'll be going out with the grocery truck on Monday night—wahoo!" Frankie gave a little shoulder shimmy and winked at Pete. "I didn't even get a break before I came here. Jason asked me to come as a favour and I didn't even get a chance to go home and get a change of clothes. These pants are really comfortable for this kind of work—this is a great job—I love making good stuff for the men—right, Stan?" She looked over her shoulder and through her bangs at him.

"You betcha," Stan quipped with a wide grin. He had filled the warming trays with hot dog buns. "Barb, do you wanna set out some ketchup and mustard on the tables? It's in the fridge at your end. I think there's some relish too, but it's in the Rec Room fridge—can you check?"

"Sure thing," I said and smiled at the air like an idiot. Maybe Stan was trying to show off how helpful I was—obedient and good at tricks. I had tried to catch Pete's eye in a friendly way, but he hadn't looked at me once. Maybe that was a step up from being despised.

"I'm almost finished peeling these potatoes, Stan. Dammit, it's hard to hold this peeler with my gloves—it keeps slipping—these are special gloves for my latex allergy. Those men are going to love these mashed potatoes with fried chicken tonight." Frankie took a breath and looked over at me. "Oh yeah, Barb, could you bring me another jug of milk from the Rec Room too?"

"Yup. I'm on my way." The door behind me closed on Stan's question to Pete, "So do you think I should give Legacy a call . . . ?"

The television was blaring to an empty Rec Room. I guessed the rest of the boys had passed out—no Herb either. The two refrigerators were near the door; I rummaged through them both until I found the relish and milk. As much as I wanted to know about the rig move, I decided to make my escape from the kitchen as soon as I could. Meanwhile, I wondered when and if Stan was going to tell Pete that I was taking Frankie's place. How much say did Pete have about Legacy staff? Maybe it was best to stay clear of Pete until Frankie was gone. Besides, I had bathrooms and laundry to do. And another letter to write.

Arms full, I backed my way through the kitchen door.

"Yeah, Barb, have you ever seen a rig move before?" Mark asked.

"No, I haven't. What's it like?" I set my armload on the counter beside the refrigerator.

"You should watch tomorrow. It'll go right by camp here. It's an impressive thing to see for the first time."

"Oh yeah," said Stan, lighting a cigarette, but it wasn't clear by his tone whether he agreed or not.

"What time do you think it'll go by?" asked Frankie, looking at Pete.

Pete shrugged his shoulders. No one seemed to want to challenge that estimate.

"Oh, you'll hear it," said Mark. He laughed. "Trevor'll be a busy boy tomorrow."

Cody grinned. He had a mouthful of hot dog.

"Do you think we'll have to move camp, Pete?" Frankie leaned with her back against the counter, the gloves finally off.

He looked up at Frankie over the mug at his lips. "Probably not. We'll see. The new site's not far away."

I mumbled something about laundry and left the kitchen. The floor felt solid, but now I knew that camps moved on a shrug.

◆

Eventually Pete left and the camp settled down for its afternoon nap. I retreated to my room and started the next letter.

Dear God,

Well, you got my attention. You must want something more for my life than I do. Here I am, still alive and sober. I know you brought me here for a reason. It's beautiful and terrible at the same time. I don't know what's going to happen to me. My life is in your hands.

I've blamed you for everything. Not anymore. You didn't make me go bankrupt, you didn't tell me to lie and get credit that I didn't deserve and couldn't pay back. I made those choices on my own. I've been so mad at you for not protecting me from myself, for not closing doors that I pushed open. Some of it I still don't understand, why things happened the way they did, and maybe I never will. Debra says that you put John in my life to keep me alive, that without him to worry about, I might have killed myself. Maybe that's true—I don't know.

I was so mad at you for the way Marguerite died. Why did so many bad things have to happen to her? Still, I have to say thank you. If Marguerite hadn't gone bankrupt in Grand Forks and moved to Courtenay, I never would have met her. No one else would have given me the time she gave me. The terrible thing that happened to Marguerite saved my life. Do the same with me.

Thank you that Melissa and Brian are safe.

In spite of everything, you've kept me sober and you got me here alive. You must have a plan. You're all I have. Please help me start my life over.

•

I closed the scribbler. There was still about an hour left before the boys would be up for showers and supper. Alone and still, my body at rest, I felt almost physically held. Where arms of flesh would have pressed, my body didn't feel so vacant, so cold. My lips tingled. Oh. I stared out the window. The draped white boughs of pine and fir. The heavy angle of sunlight and shadow. Line on line, the clarity of the season amplified the hour in me. For a time, there was nothing but the romance of what the grader had spared.

•

Later, while I mopped the hallway, folded towels and burned garbage, I thought about faith and folly. I considered the principles of heat and light, water and temperature. I imagined myself setting off down the road without Stan's coveralls or Darlene's boots and believing that I could walk to Grande Prairie trusting in the power of prayer. If I froze to death, would it be a failure of faith? Was winter God's fault if I chose to ignore warnings and expert advice? Plain common sense? Even a child knew better than that.

Finally, I got down on my knees to measure cardboard squares for the fresh doormat. It was a new puzzle every day, taping the boxes to the linoleum and then to each other. The trick was to use the folds already in the boxes and line them up with the width of the hallway. The paper towel boxes worked the best. While I adjusted and cut and taped, I drifted and daydreamed. The boxes were bandages and I was dressing a wound. My knuckles around the scissors, my fingers pressing the cut edges together: a question of healing came to me. What if I was someone who, after a long slow recovery in hospital, refused to leave the ward? While the new mat took shape, I wondered about the toxic safety of staying hurt and hidden.

$1,100

I rubbed my eyes and opened *Twenty-Four Hours a Day*. It was Saturday, January 25, and the day's reading asked, "Have I gotten over that dependence on drinking?" *Yes, I have.* Alcohol was my poison. "Any doubts?" I sat on my bunk in the lamplight and listened for an excuse to take a drink, the whisper of a maybe, a lurking "if only." *No doubts.* No matter what.

The reading went on to say that God had "many mansions." Indeed. I had to admit the campie's room was better than a couch in somebody's living room. It was better than a trailer with a broken furnace. And yes, it was even better than the bedroom of an obligated relative who wished I wasn't there and hoped I wouldn't stay. The room was half storage and half public, but it was warm, clean and free. Yes, this was far from a homeless shelter or a bed in detox.

Okay. *This is who I am and this is where I live.* Just for today, I was the sober campie at Trinidad 11.

Suddenly I remembered that I had to vacuum the Rec Room before dayshift got in there—or Herb. I put my books away quickly and pulled the wedge from underneath the door. The hallway was already smoky; Stan had the kitchen door propped open. As I walked in, Kid Rock and Sheryl Crow were still singing, *"I found your picture today. I swear I'll change my ways. I just called to say I want you to come back home . . . "*

I called out, "Morning, Stan, morning, Frankie."

Frankie was swaying in the same place. "Hi, Barb. Did you have a good sleep?"

"Morning, Barb." Stan did a two-step shuffle and spin at the grill.

"I wake up even before the alarm goes off, dammit," Frankie said and then laughed. "What time are we in here anyway—4 a.m.? I like getting a lot of work done early and then I can sleep later. These rig boxes are almost ready." She looked through her bangs and over her shoulder. "I'm catching up to you, Stan."

"You're smokin' this morning." Stan whistled a few notes and twirled a ladle over his head.

"Are you just getting up now, Barb?" Frankie called.

"Yeah, I had a good sleep, Frankie." I choked off any more words in my defense. What was the point? I measured coffee grounds into the basket and filled the coffee maker with water. The tune sexed up the floor space between Stan and Frankie's banter. "Well, I gotta vacuum that Rec Room this morning—see you guys later."

Stan tipped a flipper and Frankie raised a carrot.

◆

Like everything else in camp, the vacuum cleaner suffered from gigantism: it was an oil drum on casters with a hose wide enough to suck up a body. After I'd picked up the empties, I dragged the machine to the far end of the room and flipped the switch. The motor filled my ears and I began to waltz with a heavy partner and the memory of carpets past.

◆

I am vacuuming grey linoleum. He comes at me. I hold up the nozzle but he yanks it out of my hand. My spine hits the counter edge hard. He is yelling in my face and his hands are around my throat.

I'm vacuuming cinders that have spit out of the fireplace and burned deep into the brown carpet while the two of us are dead drunk and our babies are asleep.

I am vacuuming the new beige carpet, overwhelmed by the yardwork and the mortgage and two teenagers and court dates and how I am going to survive alone.

I am vacuuming other women's houses, making careful turns around cherrywood legs, reaching under their beds for used condoms that bung up the works.

I am vacuuming the shop for New York Nails and love the racket those chips and tips make going up the hose, the staccato of cash for groceries and gas.

I am vacuuming the ruined carpet in an empty house for the last time because the kids are gone, the tenants are gone, the furniture is gone, Marguerite is dead, and as soon as I'm done, this vacuum cleaner and all of its attachments will go to the Salvation Army.

◆

Finished. I towed the machine back to the campie's room and coiled the hose like a fat rattler in a dark corner. I had to get those sheets ready, but the boys were still in bed

◆

The dayshift boys trundled out the door behind Herb. Meanwhile, I had made the rounds for garbage and geared up. It was dark—8:30 a.m. The late daylight still surprised me. So did the stars. I couldn't get over them, every morning, suspended points of light on the end of my gloved fingertips.

The incinerator went to work; the metal stack pinged and groaned in the frigid air. From where I was standing, the camp looked like a giant's shoebox. Bars of window light shot across the snow. *Pop off the lid.* I knew those floors with my knuckles and knees, which uneven corners trapped gunk, the slant of the hallway between Roughnecks and Room 6. I knew Old Tom staggered out the door drunk to earn more in one day than I could in six days. The garbage chattered in the fire and sent ash high over my head. I knew it wasn't fair to compare our wages. Who knew what kind of a life he'd had or what horrors were in his dark corners. Tom was close in build and weight to me—small for a riggie. He might not be as old as he looked. His hair was still thick and black, and when I looked beyond *drunk* and the hard lines of climate, I saw dark blue eyes, the nose and jaw of a man who had probably been handsome. I wondered what his days were like at the rig with Pete and the boys. No. It wasn't fair. I didn't want to be Tom and, probably, neither did he.

◆

Two hours later, Stan yelled, "How do you like your steak, Barb?"

"Huh?" I was still in the hallway, pulling off his coveralls from my second garbage trip, this one in the daylight. I tossed the gloves and toque onto my bed. Somebody had moved the stuff on my desk and left the door open. Stan, I guessed.

Frankie saw me come into the kitchen. "We're having a barbecue tonight," she called. "Stan's doing steaks. The boys are gonna love this—I know Mark said he loves steak."

"Fuck 'em if they don't," hollered Stan. Frankie had the sink taps wide open.

"A barbecue in the snow?" I was more interested in the laundry bins: time for the next load. The T-bones were set out in a long row to thaw along Stan's counter space. They looked almost decorative. As for Stan, he was stoned.

"Hell yeah, right at the back door." Stan laughed. "This is camp, you know, the Saturday night dinner special. They get steak once a week, and I do a mean *barb-e-cue*." He laughed again, cigarette in one hand and bottled steak sauce in the other. "Come on, I'll show you." He waved the bottle at me and yanked the back door open.

"Yeah, you should see it, Barb." Frankie pointed at the door. "He got Dave to set it up for us. It's gonna be great. Party tonight—wahoo!" She waved a dishcloth at me. "Go on, check it out."

The both of them had red glassy eyes and big fat grins. It wasn't even 10:00 a.m. "I'll get my boots," I said, hoping to buy time and get lost.

"Nah," Stan snorted. "You've got runners on—come on and see this."

What was the big deal about a barbecue? Had these two idiots never seen one before? Stan waited. I stopped at the door and looked over at Frankie: big smile. Okay.

"Go." He bowed low and waved his arm for me to pass.

I nodded and stepped over the threshold. The sky was clear, the temperature around −20 in the sunshine. Sure enough, there was a big propane barbecue set up on a plywood pallet in the snow.

"Wow. Cool."

Stan stood on the landing, grinning. "I'm doing baked potatoes with all the fixin's. It's gonna be great."

"Yeah—boy, I can't wait." Then I jumped back onto the top step. Stan stared at the barbecue. A cigarette hung from his lip. "Come on, Stan. Let's go back inside—it's cold out here."

He stirred. "What? Cold? Shit no." He waved at the sky and laughed. "Are you kidding? This is *barb-e-cue* weather." Then he flicked his cigarette into the snow and followed me back inside.

"Dammit, isn't that barbecue cool?" Frankie brushed her bangs aside with her forearm. "We never had anything like that at the other camp. I think Pete brought it over for us. Don't you think the weather's perfect for a barbecue? I wanted to do up a potato salad to go with the steaks but Stan wants baked potatoes instead. I think we should do both. Then the guys can have a choice of whatever they want." Frankie bent over the sink, the tops of her special blue non-latex gloves barely visible over the soap bubbles. "Oh, and we've got corn on the cob too!"

"And don't forget the pie," said Stan. He leaned against the counter across from Frankie, his arms crossed, tunic unbuttoned. "Cherry."

"Yum-me," said Frankie. She licked her lips and looked over her shoulder at Stan, grinning.

"I gotta check the laundry. See you guys in a bit."

Get a grip. Stan and Frankie had the munchies. I'd forgotten about those 3:00 a.m. trips to all-night restaurants. They were high and having fun. As for me, well, I looked like a stuck-up prude. Really, I was afraid of things that threatened my life—in particular, getting high, cherry pie and barbecues.

◆

The kitchen was quiet except for the mop and rusty wheels on the bucket. Lunch was over; Stan and Frankie had disappeared, as usual. I had stacked all the chairs on the tables and rolled up the heavy black mats in front of the sinks. I pushed laundry bins out of the way and washed deep into the corners around the cupboards. One hand pushed, the other hand pulled. I wondered if Frankie was giving Stan a tug right now. Had Stan phoned Legacy about my job yet? Where would I be this time next month? Next week? Outside, the crows and ravens were going at it.

By the time I reached the doorway, the other end of the room was dry. I carefully towed the bucket down the hallway to the laundry sink. It was an awkward lift and twist to get the hot slopping water down the drain. Usually I got soaked. Today was usual.

I kicked the wedge under the campie's door so I could change my wet clothes. Through the blinds, slices of blue sky tantalized me. In the suitcase, my scribbler. I'd saved the last letter for the worst offender: me. This was probably the best time to write, especially with Stan and Frankie's Saturday night plans for the camp dinner. With one last look through the blinds, I opened the scribbler and sat down at the desk. My fingers cradled the pen over the blank page.

Dear Barbara,
You're the one I've had it in for—the biggest betrayal of all, and the hardest to forgive. Who did you think you were? Look at

where you are now. Somehow, I have to forgive you because my sobriety and my life depend on it. If I don't find some way of making peace with you, I'll never get over this. I won't survive.

You destroyed everything I worked so hard to save. That's what I hear in my thoughts, over and over. You wrecked your own life. All the while praying for God's guidance and going to meetings. Is that true? No. Not everything is lost. You didn't drink. You didn't do any of John's heroin. You didn't kill yourself or anyone else. Face it. What you lost was money.

You lied. You knew. And yet you kept right on going until you landed on your ass out in the snow. Literally! You threw away things I cared about. You threw away my chance to get ahead. I think God brought me here to face you.

I know that you were in so much pain and on so much Prozac that you couldn't think straight. I know there are blank spots of memory, whole days, weeks, that you can't remember what you did or who you were with. You were sick and in grief and all the bad things that you'd been holding back came out. But you never told anyone the whole truth. You just wouldn't break down.

I don't understand but I forgive you. I release you from all the blame and judgment for everything that's happened. You still have your sobriety, your health and some brains. You can still write. This is hell but I know that you're not going to stay here. I know you tried hard to do something good. Start again.

◆

I needed to get to the bathroom and wash my wrecked face without anybody seeing me. Scribbler hidden back in the suitcase, I listened at the door. Still quiet. I ran for it: past the Rec Room, left and left again. Ladies' bathroom—home free—the only door with a lock. Cool water felt good on my swollen eyes; I looked up at the mirror. *Hello in there.* Something in my chest moved.

◆

The snow was like white flour with just the right amount of lard worked into it: not solid but not powder. It held its shape but fell apart at a touch. A look. A glare. If I put a twist to my step, it squelched. Squeaked. Spoke. Deeper, a foot or so underneath the loose snow, was hard ice.

I'd made another exit from camp in a new direction. The skies were clear but the weather report had predicted snow later. When I turned left onto the main road, I was moving face first into the wind. The temperature was –26 and falling. I'd had in mind to walk toward Beaver camp. I wasn't sure how far it was and doubted that I'd have time to get there, but at least it was a destination. So far, no traffic, only the ravens overhead. The birds were so black and big, it was almost a reflex to look for the impress of their calls in the snow, as if their language left tracks.

The road rose and fell rapidly; it wasn't long before I was breathing deeply. Ice crystals blew up into my face. There wasn't much of it exposed, but my eyes were already stinging. I'd zipped Stan's coveralls well past my chin and over my nose, lowered the toque and hood as far as I could. Still, it wasn't long before I turned back to walk with the wind. It was quiet; it was loud. The tree lines seemed to me a wilderness script against the sky, God's handwritten language in colour and cold. Out here, nothing seemed more important than absorbing the vocabulary all around me.

◆

Stan was fussing with the steaks, poking at them with a fork, turning them in deep pans of marinade. Frankie was wrapping potatoes in tinfoil while she hummed *I been waitin' on you for a long time, fuelin' up on heartaches and cheap wine . . .*

I'd finished cleaning four bathrooms and was looking for an excuse to go outside again. The slouch, the smile, Stan and Frankie looked too relaxed.

"Hey, Frankie, I think I'll grab that garbage before those peelings get too heavy."

"Oh sure," she said and glanced in my direction. "Did you go out for your walk, Barb?"

"Yeah, but that wind picked up, so I didn't go far."

"I had a great sleep—I feel really good. How many more potatoes do you think I should do, Stan?"

He looked up from the meat. "Oh hell, another dozen or so. We might get company. I think Pete's coming later, and maybe some of the other guys with him."

"Oh yeah, the rig move today," said Frankie, dumping more potatoes into the sink.

"Besides, I can always use the extras for breakfast tomorrow—fry 'em up. The boys love them."

"Me too," quipped Frankie.

"Heading outside again, Barb?" asked Stan.

I stood there with two full black plastic garbage bags. And if he said *barb-e-cue* one more time . . . "Yup."

"You'll see the rig go by," Stan said and then smiled, "but it'll be a while yet. Don't forget there's that big hill. That's probably where the rig's at—you can hear it now. They're trying to bring it up the hill," he explained. "Don't worry." He laughed. "You won't miss it."

I was worried. Here was a chance to see something I'd never seen before, and up close. What if the rig went down the road while I was changing the beds?

"Yeah, don't worry, Barb." Frankie nodded benevolently over a vat of coleslaw. "I've seen lots of rigs. Dammit, are we going to have to move camp, Stan?"

"I don't think so. Legacy hasn't said anything."

I left their chatter to fold towels. Even inside camp, the engine roar was louder, but there was still nothing in sight. Over the next hour I washed the hallway floors, tidied the pantry shelves and made a new mat for the backdoor. All the while, the noise got louder and louder until, finally, I ran to the back door. There it was—the rig.

Three identical semi-tractors pulled the horizontal tower. They rolled forward in single inches. I'd never seen anything like it—that much power in one place, doing one thing. Behind the tower, a fourth semi-tractor pushed. It was Stan's leverage to the max. I wanted to throw candy, jump up and down and wave.

The driver in the first truck was a dark figure at the wheel—I wondered if it was Trevor. The tower itself was a framework of criss-crossing bars and blue geometry. The convoy filled the white road against the backdrop of evergreens under the puny sky. Compression reverberated through my body, the sound waves almost palpable, almost visible, a mechanical reckoning of purpose. Fuel perfumed the air. I felt an inner lurch, a sudden yearning to be part of the energy that controlled those massive engines. Yet the true source of the power was as unreal to me as I was nothing to it.

"Whoa, there it is," Frankie yelled right behind me.

"Yup. That's it." Stan leaned over Frankie's shoulder and exhaled smoke into her ear.

I made room for both of them on the step. The three of us stood in the sunlight, practically shoulder to shoulder, and watched the rig. We yelled and used goofy hand gestures to complete our sentences, our calls lost to the engines.

It was the first time I'd seen Frankie outside the camp building. She squinted and used her hand as a visor against the sunlight. Her hair shone, and I noticed her skin and teeth were still good.

Stan looked even worse in sunlight, skin like an old yellow onion. In a few years he'd be almost parchment. He saw me looking at him and pointed with his thumb to the door. I got it and so did Frankie.

◆

The boys lined up early for their steaks.

"How'll you have your steak, Pete?" Stan waved his fork like a wand over the grill and speared a steak from the flame. "Here you go, Cody. Medium-well, right? Corn, potatoes in the kitchen. What's that, Pete? Rare? You got it. Eric? You did say 'medium,' eh? She's ready for you now—grab 'er while she's dripping." He lifted a steak and dropped it onto Mark's plate.

Dan, Eric, Pete and some of the others stood in the snow with loose-laced boots and open jackets, as if they'd just cut the lawn and were comparing mowers. They all held travel mugs but not for coffee.

By now I had figured out that "dry camp" meant "not obviously wet." As soon as they got their steak, one by one they stomped back up the stairs and into the kitchen to eat.

"Barb, how'll you have it?" Stan asked.

Pete caught the question and scowled in my direction.

"Medium-well, thanks, Stan."

"Here's one ready." Stan motioned for my plate.

Back inside, the kitchen was a pudding of smoke and noise. The boys yelled at each other over the radio, over Frankie's high hoots and Stan's "come-and-get-it" steak calls. I had planned to eat in my room. I really wished I could eat in my car. The whole place was Saturday night slippery, everybody greased with booze and dope, the jaw's great lubricant. My head ached, my throat hurt. I broke the rule and took my food to my room, unnoticed. Laughter pierced the closed door and sharpened my own silence. The steak was tough chewing, unevenly burnt and raw. But the baked potato was good, the starch told my belly that my heart was full.

A few hours later I dragged the bags of kitchen garbage across the snow. Dinner plates and meaty T-bones flashed through the warm slop I pushed into the mouth of the incinerator. It all smelled pretty good, and I didn't plan to hang around out here for any longer than it took to slam the door, turn the dial and run back to the building. The bear with a "head as big as an oil barrel" kept tapping me on the back.

Meanwhile, camp had coagulated into an all-out Saturday night party. Somehow, I had to wash the kitchen floor—it was in bad shape from the barbecue boys. My eyes were burning and my back hurt. It was 10:00 p.m. when I put the kitchen to bed.

On my last trip to the bathroom, I passed Blake in the hallway. He probably thought I was the one on a slant. The Rec Room door opened and closed, and in that brief blast I heard Frankie's laughter mixed with manly howls. I hoped she'd be okay in there. She would have laughed at my hope.

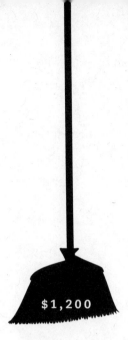

$1,200

I pulled out my earplugs. Not a sound. I sniffed the air. No coffee, no bacon. Something was wrong. My room was okay, the shelves in order, the door still wedged shut. The clock: Sunday, 5:00 a.m. I sat on the edge of the bunk and debated what to do. *It's a camp holiday?* I'd slept a little later than usual. Maybe by the time I got dressed I'd hear the normal breakfast racket. *They're all dead?* If what I suspected had happened, Stan and Frankie might as well be.

It crossed my mind to wait and see what would happen to Stan if the boys staggered into a cold empty kitchen. *No.* I pulled on my sweats, rolled away the blankets, yanked out the wedge and opened the door. The hallway was empty. So was the kitchen. I passed the barren counters almost at a run and turned down the hallway to the door labelled *Cook.*

"Stan? It's Barb. Hello? Good morning . . . are you awake?" It might have been on my third rap. The door dematerialized under my knuckles and Stan erupted from the room, his startled tunic flapping from his chest like white wings. I followed his tailwind back to the kitchen.

He plunged into the fridge and spun around to face me with an armful of bacon and eggs. "Could you go bang on Frankie's door?" His face was ashen, eyeballs hard and glassy.

"Okay." I hustled back down the hallway and then stopped short. Pete's dog was asleep at Frankie's door.

Back in the kitchen, Stan was hotfooting it from the counter to the stove to the fridge and back again.

"Is she coming?" he asked.

"Pete's dog is at her door."

At first he didn't say anything, just kept whisking the eggs. Then he looked up. "Fuck." Neither one of us was going to touch Frankie's door.

"I'll put on the coffee and then tell me what to do."

His hands were full. He pointed with his foot. "Pull out those rig boxes . . . there's some ham in the fridge. You can use that to make sandwiches. And then cut up some cheese." Whisk poised, he craned his neck to see the dessert shelf. "Wrap up some of those lemon squares too." Then he went back to work, double time.

For a while we worked together in silence, back to back, focusing on the clock and not chopping off a fingertip. The kitchen door opened. We both looked up—no Frankie. Dan gave me a sour look, poured a coffee and left without speaking. The boys were cranky.

Stan cracked. "She's outta here today. She's gone." He jerked his head at the counter in front of me. "You can start today. When she gets up, I'm gonna tell her to pack up her shit and go home."

"What about Legacy? Are you going to phone Jason?"

"I'll call right after breakfast." He was two-handing it to catch up— flipper for the hash browns, the other hand for salt and pepper, pushing bacon, flicking ash from the cigarette between his teeth.

"How will she get out of here?" I worried about a long messy ending.

"Legacy'll drive her out when they bring in a replacement."

I wrapped the lemon squares in cellophane and worried anyway. Job switch or not, there were still morning chores, the Rec Room and laundry, beds to change. Every time I heard a door slam, I jumped and looked for Frankie to come a-swinging into the kitchen. "Dammit," she'd say. I wondered if Pete would come in for breakfast. I imagined Mrs. Pete explaining that poor daddy had to stay out and work all night.

"Morning, Cody. How'll you have your eggs this morning—scrambled?" Stan smiled at the hungover kid who came through the door next. Cody mumbled an answer. He didn't seem to notice Frankie's replacement.

"Hi, Cody," I said. "Stan, these rig boxes are ready to go."

"Great. Leave them there and I'll get Herb to carry them out."

The door opened again—Eric and Dan. They both looked over and nodded at me without expression. I realized that I was probably the only employee blind and deaf to the night's pairing. "Hey, guys," Stan called and walked over to talk with them.

"I'm going to burn the kitchen garbage and then get the laundry going, Stan. See you in a bit . . . unless you need me for anything else."

"No. Go ahead . . . and thanks." He gave me a half smile, half shrug, and turned back to Eric and Dan. The three of them were still mumbling in a huddle when I clomped down the stairs and tromped through the snow, dragging carrot peelings and celery sticks, the undigested aches and pains of Frankie's hands and feet under the dark morning sky.

◆

The first offering of the day sizzled and popped. I stood there alone, mute under the din of stars. My shoulders dropped. *I surrender* . . . a heaviness released . . . *my broken heart* . . . through my arms and legs . . . *all my shame* . . . and fell into the snow . . . *to you.* The icy air cupped the heat of my face in its smoky, fragrant hands. For a moment I was the only living soul on earth. Every cell in my body felt it: beheld.

A diesel engine broke the silence and ended my prayer. Over in the parking lot, the crew cab idled in a cloud of exhaust while Herb waited for the dayshift boys to come out. One last deep lung-full of glory before I turned to follow my tracks back to camp. I wondered what the boys would talk about on their way to the rig this morning. I wondered if Frankie had a job as long as she stayed in bed with Pete. Whatever happened, at least now I didn't have to worry about bed and board. I could still hear the Quesnel social worker's blunt words when she'd handed me the emergency relief cheque. "Don't come back here." I'd sworn never to face that humiliation again. The camp door slammed shut, audible emphasis to the vow. Ahead, long elastic shadows lumbered across the snow toward the crew cab.

Back inside the kitchen, still no Frankie. Stan heard me and poked his head around the door. "Can you give me a hand in here? The dishes are piling up."

"Okay." I dumped my boots and detoured my chores from the laundry. He wasn't kidding—both sinks were full. Frankie's special non-latex gloves waited like Pete's dog. I found another pair and strong-armed the sprayer to rinse the plates. For the next hour I scrubbed, picked, chunked, stabbed and scoured. My back was to Stan and the row of windows. The world of the cook's helper was the length of the sinks plus about three feet of counter space. The higher-than-standard counters pinched the vertical air space to about 20 inches from the overhead cupboards. Pale yellow paint brightened the shallow vista of dishwater and a blank wall.

Dave came into the kitchen. He walked over to Stan, said something and then left. I waited for an update.

Stan rolled his eyes. "Frankie's buggered off with Pete—he's taken her with him down to the rig."

"Is she coming back?"

"I'll tell you in a minute." Stan dropped the cloth in his hand and left the kitchen. I was drying the same pan when he came back. "Her stuff's still here—she'll be back."

"Okay." There wasn't much else to say and there was a heap of dishes to dry. Behind me, Stan was scouring the grill. We worked without speaking until Stan broke the silence.

"So what religion are you?"

His question startled me. I hesitated before answering. How much did I want to reveal? "Umm, well . . . I guess you could say I'm Anglican. But I've been lots of other things too—United, Baptist, Nazarene, Pentecostal," and then, as if to further weaken my spiritual convictions, "I was almost a Catholic."

"Oh yeah," Stan said flatly. His tone said *I thought as much.*

My towel was sopping wet. I grabbed a dry one and lifted another bowl to wipe. I didn't speak.

"I was an altar boy. My dad was big in the Catholic Church—I mean big, *real big*."

"Oh really?"

"Yup. And I was an altar boy in the church—I did it for *years*." It was classic Stan, his voice and vocabulary spiced with ambiguity. He never broke the rhythm of scouring the steel grill plates, and for a time there was no other sound in the kitchen.

What do you want me to say to him? Nothing. Stan scoured and I listened.

It wasn't long before the kitchen door opened. We both stopped and looked. Dave leaned in and said, "Pete's back with Frankie. She's coming in."

That was my cue to get lost. I didn't want any part of a scene between Stan and Frankie. "I better check the dryer," I said and put down the dishcloth.

Stan nodded. "Sure." And this time, he looked sure.

I didn't see Frankie come inside the camp. After the laundry, I carried on with the campie's chores. I never heard a raised voice. In fact, the camp was unusually quiet—severely hungover, I assumed. Or everyone, like me, was waiting to see what happened next between Pete and Frankie.

When I finished the bathrooms, I remembered my letters. The timing seemed perfect. Back in my room I tore the pages out of the scribbler and folded them into the pockets of Stan's coveralls.

The day had dawned brilliant, without cloud or wind. No one saw me trudge across the parking lot to the incinerator. Only a white-gowned host of trees witnessed my repentance. I opened the door with my letters in hand. "These are for you, God. I'm ready to start over with your help." Then I put the letters inside on the black ash, closed the door, turned the dial. The smoke rose straight out of the stack in a solid white line against the blue sky. It pleased me to see my words lift, transformed, in the air. Eventually a high breeze caught the smoke line and bent it, almost at a right angle. I stepped back and watched the line cross the parking lot, directly over the vehicles, over the Toyota.

A ridiculous thought came to me. *You should see if the car will start.* I left the incinerator and walked over to the car, encased again by a thick shell of snow and ice. As I had done before in Grande Prairie, I used my body to push off the snow and find the door handle. Against my better judgment, I pulled hard and opened the door, risking damage to the frozen hinges. And then, for no reason that made sense, I got inside the car and sat behind the wheel. A shadow fell over me.

"You'd better see if you can get it started."

I jumped. It was Stan. I had to shield my eyes from the sunlight to see him.

"What?"

"You'd better see if you can get it started. You're fired."

"What?" I felt the cold air on my teeth. My mouth was gaping.

"Frankie told Pete that you and I were being mean to her. So Pete phoned Legacy this morning from the rig. They just phoned me. We're both fired. Our replacements will be here in a couple of hours. Pack up. You're leaving."

I sat in the car, hand over my eyes, and looked at Stan. Directly over his head I saw the smoke line. My work was finished. It was time to go home.

Stan waited for me, probably still in shock himself. I got out of the car and pushed the door shut. He shivered, arms crossed tight against his chest. No coat—I guessed he'd answered the phone and run out the door looking for me. He must have been waiting for my reaction. I smiled at the blue sky and the drifting line of smoke. I smiled at Stan's pale face and said, "Okay."

◆

It didn't take long to pack. I finished the laundry but left the garbage. There was no sign of Frankie. None of the boys I passed in the kitchen or hallways said anything, just nodded and looked away. The next thing I knew there was a Jeep in the parking lot with a new cook and two young replacements at the door. As we had done on my first day, Stan called a staff meeting in the cook's bedroom. The new cook was an eager woman who I guessed to be in her late 40s, brown hair in a dated bouffant. She looked solid, not fat; she was grilling Stan about the next meal due. The cook's helper and camp attendant were two girls. I doubted they were more than 19 years old, with long tangled hair, tie-dyed T-shirts. They slumped on Stan's bed against the wall, barely conscious, their faces turned away from me. It was almost noon.

Stan paused from his review of the menu with the new cook. "Barb, could you show Chrissie the ropes? You know, show her what Andy showed you?"

"Sure, glad to." I looked at the curvy hips and legs now sprawled across the bed. "We'd better do it now, because I want to get to Grande Prairie before dark." I directed my voice to the girl. "Are you ready, Chrissie?"

"Yeah." She pulled herself upright, tugged at her T-shirt, pushed her hair away from her face and looked at me. "Let's do it."

And so I did, ran through the bathrooms, the floors, the cardboard matting, the laundry, the Rec Room; showed her how to change the sheets and clean the rooms. Garbage I saved for the best and for the last. We stood in the sunlight. Poor Chrissie, almost blinded, had hardly said more than two words, trying to take in my instructions. Or suffer them, ignore them, fuck them, I wasn't sure; her eyes were unfocused.

"Well, that's about it. Any questions?"

She looked at me. Her face needed a wash; there were tide lines of eye makeup on her cheeks. I wanted to grab her shoulders, warn her about the dangers in camp, about a life that could grind a woman down and then toss her out on her ass in the snow. Isabel had warned me about Old Tom; now I wanted to warn Chrissie about . . . what? All the Toms? I wanted to tell her something more important than how to make a bed.

"Nope." She scowled. "We done?"

"That's it. Good luck." I stuck out my hand. At first she didn't see it, or maybe she didn't know what to do with it; the gesture seemed foreign to her. Finally she took my hand and I shook her weak grip. "Well, I'm gonna see about getting my car started."

We had our roles, and the urge to trespass—well, she'd probably think I was nuts or had been too long in camp.

Chrissie followed me back into the campie's room. I hauled my suitcase off the bed and stood it at the back door. The Jeep driver came out of the kitchen. He was a tall thin man wearing a ball jacket and cap.

"I'm Mark, from Legacy," he said briskly. "We're leaving now. Are you ready to go?"

"What?"

"I'm driving you all back to Grande Prairie—you and Frankie. We gotta get going."

"No, I don't need a ride. I've got my car here. I just need someone to help me get it started."

"Well, hurry up. The weather's turning and I want to leave now. Get your stuff"—he jerked his head at my suitcase—"and you can follow me out to the highway." He turned to walk away.

"Wait a minute, I can't go yet. My car's still frozen." I saw his look— pissed off. "I'm not leaving my car here."

He shrugged his shoulders.

I got it: *Not my problem, sister.* "I'm not leaving without my car. I can't. Besides, if I go off the road, are you going to help me get it out?"

"No."

"Then leave. Don't wait for me. I'll drive out on my own."

"See ya." He turned around and went into the kitchen.

I walked past my old room. The door was wide open. Chrissie was on the bed; a girl sprawled out and wasted for all the world to see.

◆

Where was Stan? I wanted to say goodbye and ask him to help me start my car. Maybe he was in the Rec Room. I pushed the door open and a bar of light shot into the dark room. The lights were off. That was odd. I couldn't find the switch, so I wedged the door open behind me. When I turned around, Frankie was standing in the middle of the room, alone in the dark. Black lines of mascara streaked her face, and her eyes were swollen and red. She looked like she didn't know where she was.

"Frankie? It's Barb—it's me."

"Oh . . . I'm . . . I'm . . . " She blinked at the light.

"Frankie, are you okay?"

"Where's . . . where's . . . I was with him . . . where's . . . um . . . ?"

"Where's . . . Pete?"

"Yes. Where's Pete?"

"He's gone, Frankie. He's not here."

"Who was . . . ?" Her face contorted. Her shoulders shook, head fell to her chest, whole body convulsed. She sobbed, deep gut-wrenching sobs.

"It was Pete, Frankie. His name was Pete." She must have figured it out when the new Legacy staff showed up and what's-his-name was nowhere in sight. He must have promised to come back for her and that's why she was waiting here in the dark—to avoid having to face Stan and me. My heart broke. She had worked for 12 days straight to be the kind of woman they wanted in camp. I wanted to put my hand on her shoulder, but something held me back. We stood within inches of each other in that suffocating room, yet my arm wouldn't reach that far.

Frankie caught her breath. "I'm so sorry, Barb." She raised her hands to her face and slowly shook her head, still crying.

"It doesn't matter, Frankie. Don't worry. I'll be okay."

Again, I found myself full of urgency, yet stifled, unable to speak. I wanted to say that I was sorry. That I was sorry for being a coward, for hiding in my room and not being honest about who I was and why I was there. I hadn't been able to overcome my fear of the boys and the booze, and I had never found a way to let her know I wasn't a threat. Now that wasn't true either. Maybe being unable to console Frankie was finally the truth—I was not her friend.

But neither was I her enemy.

A shadow blocked the light. It was Mark. "There you are. Come on—let's go."

"Okay, I'm coming." Frankie looked at me. Her eyes were shiny red slits, cheeks smeared with snot and tears, face wrecked.

"Goodbye, Frankie."

"Bye, Barb," she whispered, her mouth twisted. Then she rubbed her face with the back of her sleeve and left the room.

For a moment I couldn't move, hating the dark, but unable yet to face the light. Frankie's trauma held me. How do we survive what we do to survive? My balm wouldn't heal her anguish. It only worked when you knew nothing else would. This was not some mystical dimension and it was more than a mark on a grid. Camp was a real place of isolation and danger. The date was Sunday, January 26, 2003, and the time was just after 1:00 p.m. We were somewhere in the wilderness south-west of Grande Prairie, Alberta, at an oil-rig camp called Trinidad 11. We were both fired.

♦

I found Stan. And he'd found somebody with a blowtorch who was willing to crawl underneath the Toyota and thaw it out. After a couple of tries, it started. I let the car idle while I shook Stan's hand and said goodbye.

"I already got another job to go to now or I'd guide you out," said Stan.

"I'll be fine," I said.

Stan glanced up at the darkening sky. "Drive careful." He saluted and walked away.

A solid black wall was closing down on the blue sky. It was 2:00 p.m. As long as I didn't take any long detours or get completely lost, I hoped to make Grande Prairie by suppertime. There was still enough money for an overnight hotel and gas to Quesnel the next day. With one last look at camp, I pulled out of the parking lot, the Toyota growling and rocking over the frozen ruts. The car was a tank.

The first turn was easy and so was the second. I passed Beaver camp and then saw the triple rig lights. In the rear-view mirror, black clouds loomed. The last thing I wanted was to be on this road in a blizzard at night. The flashlight was on the seat beside me; I had half a tank of gas and Aunty Madge's candle in the glovebox. An hour passed without my seeing another vehicle. *It's Sunday*, I reasoned, *that's why there's no traffic. Or maybe it's because I'm on the wrong road.*

Finally the road flattened out. I was certain this was the last long stretch before a turn, a hill and then the highway. There'd been a couple of guesses, a few quick prayers, plenty of opportunities to go the wrong way. But this stretch had a familiar feel to it. So I was barrelling along, half hypnotized by the white road, daydreaming about potato chips and a long hot bath, when up ahead I saw a truck stopped at an intersection. I slowed. It was a white medical van with a big red cross on the side. For a few seconds I debated stopping to ask if I was on the right road. As I passed, I leaned forward to catch a glimpse of the driver. Two men in the truck did the same.

Not a chance. My foot pressed on the gas. *Who knows who they are?* It wasn't safe to get out of the car.

Five kilometres later, at a widening of the road, I slowed the car, turned around and drove back. Why was the truck sitting there? I couldn't get it out of my mind. What if this was the wrong road? The debate overpowered me. I drove as fast as I dared on the snow and ice. Most likely the truck was already gone. Other roads yawned open. The double-back would get me lost. *Stop looking at the gas gauge.* This was probably a waste of valuable time.

The truck was still there. I pulled up alongside and rolled down my window. The driver did the same. I pointed in the direction that I had come from. "Is this the right road back to the highway?"

The man at the wheel had a sandwich in his hand. "No. It's this one." He pointed to the right.

"Are you sure?"

"Yes. That's the road—you have to turn here. This road goes off for miles, nowhere."

"You're absolutely sure?"

"I drive this route every week," he said. "That's the way back to the highway."

"Thanks."

He waved a hand. I backed up and made the turn. The road curved and twisted for a few kilometres and suddenly intersected Highway 43. I turned left and drove north, a seamless line of black cloud at the Toyota's rear bumper.

Less than two weeks earlier, I'd made this trip with Stan. And now, just like that, it was over. I had survived the journey, worked long hard hours and stayed sober. As for Quesnel, I already knew that I wouldn't be staying there. I was going south to see my daughter and son, to tell them that I loved them. After that, who knew? There had been letters in the snow and a signal fire in the wilderness.

ACKNOWLEDGEMENTS

This book would have remained a box of scribbled notes, some matchbook covers and a length of string if not for the incredible support and editorial wisdom I received from Lynne Van Luven, Associate Dean of Fine Arts at the University of Victoria. I would also like to thank Professor David Leach and my fellow Writing 416ers for their workshop comments that helped to shape the early chapters.

I am deeply grateful to Vivian Sinclair, managing editor of Heritage House in Victoria, for her profound belief in the value of this northern story and in my ability to tell it; also, to Neil Wedin and Melva McLean for their enthusiasm; to Jacqui Thomas for her design talents; and to Audrey McClellan for her expert line-by-line editorial work on the manuscript.

Thank you, Debra Doerksen, for your fierce friendship and unwavering belief in this story and the stories I've yet to write, for your patient listening and countless readings, your truthful, courageous, poetic heart.

My deepest gratitude to Barbara Colebrook Peace and Terry Peace, whose abiding love and brave editorial insights helped me know where the story began and what was important to tell.

So many friends have helped me in practical and prayerful ways: Marie Kaleka, Gail Patterson, Dalene Paine, Leslie McCormick, Mike McCormick, Linda Willard, Hilary Cleverly, Anne Hine, and my neighbours at Mount Douglas Court.

"There's a bedroom door up here with your name on it," said Uncle Rob. I would like to thank my family for years of love and generous support: my mother, Irene Stewart; my sister, Bernice Yeadon; and my brother, David Stewart. And to my Quesnel cousins: deepest gratitude for the legacy of their mother and my aunt, Madge Heppner.

Finally, and most important, I thank God for my daughter, Melissa, and my son, Brian, the highest calling and joys of my life.

◆

The book I read in camp, *How to Stop the Pain*, was written by Dr. James B. Richards (Whitaker House, 2001). *Twenty-Four Hours a Day* was published by the Hazelden Foundation (Hazelden, 1992). The names of the men and women I worked with at Trinidad 11 have been changed.

Barbara Stewart grew up in Surrey, BC. She has worked as a banker, homemaker, housecleaner, nail girl and furniture salesperson. Soon after her stint as a campie, Barbara went to work at Heart House, a bed-and-breakfast for heart patients and their families. In 2006 she decided to return to university, and in 2010 she graduated with a Bachelor of Arts (With Distinction) from the University of Victoria's Writing Program. She has been published in *Event*, *Grain* and *The Walrus* and was shortlisted in the CBC Literary Awards competition for non-fiction (2008) and the *Event* Creative Non-fiction Contest (2009). While Barbara works on her second book, she serves on the editorial board for *The Malahat Review* and plans to complete an MFA.